Easy Piano
CARTOON TUNES 3rd Edition

T0061489

Based on the "Winnie the Pooh" works, by A.A. Milne and E.H. Shepard

ISBN 978-1-5400-2960-7

HAL•LEONARD®

Visit Hal Leonard Online at
www.halleonard.com

Contact Us:
Hal Leonard
7777 West Bluemound Road
Milwaukee, WI 53213
Email: info@halleonard.com

In Europe contact:
Hal Leonard Europe Limited
42 Wigmore Street
Marylebone, London, W1U 2RN
Email: info@halleonardeurope.com

In Australia contact:
Hal Leonard Australia Pty. Ltd.
4 Lentara Court
Cheltenham, Victoria, 3192 Australia
Email: info@halleonard.com.au

ANIMAL MECHANICALS-THEME

from the Cartoon Television Series

Words and Music by
JEFF ROSEN

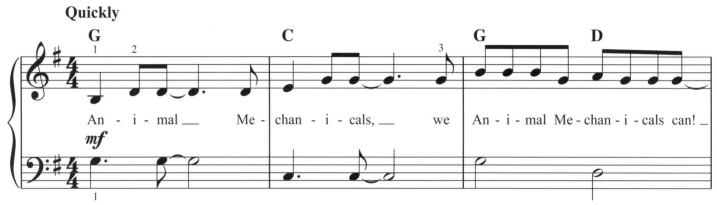

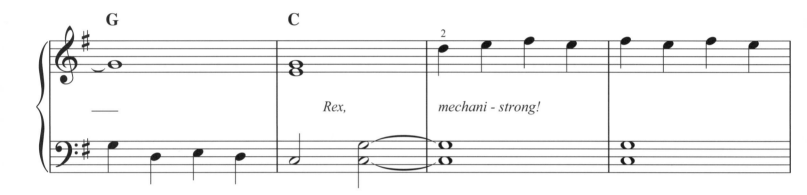

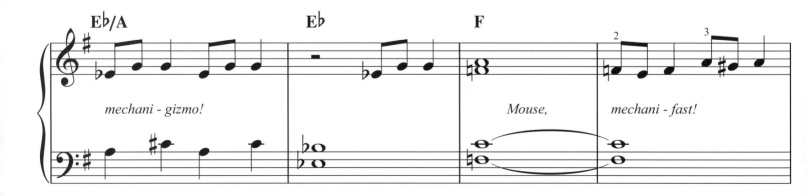

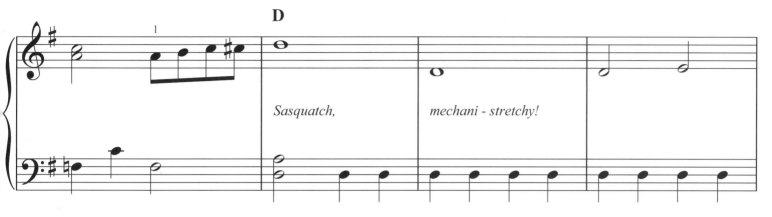

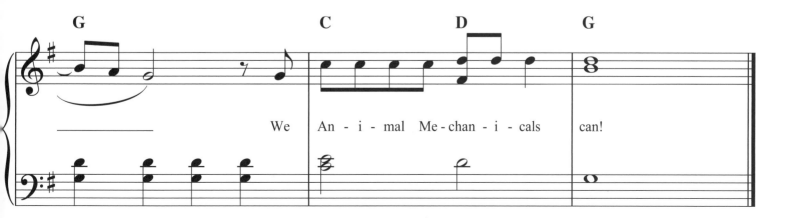

BOB THE BUILDER
(Main Title)

Words and Music by
PAUL K. JOYCE

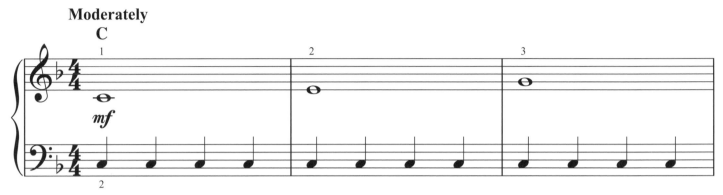

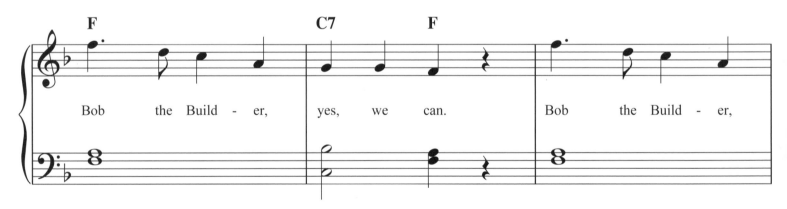

Bob the Build - er, can we fix it?
Bob the Build - er, yes, we can. Bob the Build - er,

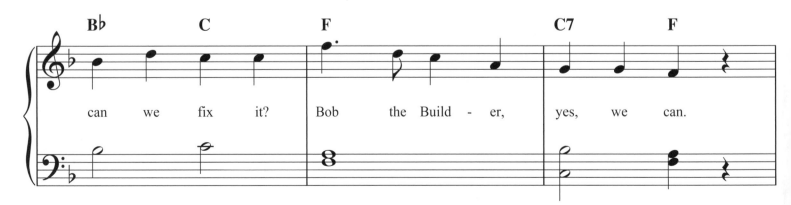

can we fix it? Bob the Build - er, yes, we can.

To Coda

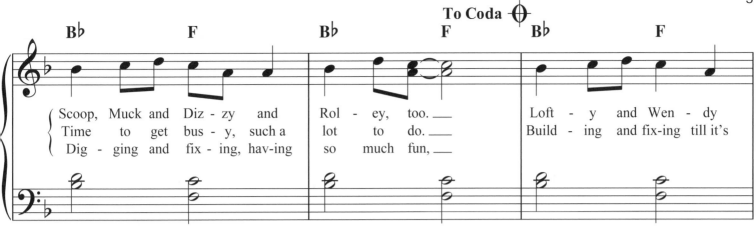

Scoop, Muck and Diz - zy and Rol - ey, too. ___ Loft - y and Wen - dy
Time to get bus - y, such a lot to do. ___ Build - ing and fix-ing till it's
Dig - ging and fix - ing, hav-ing so much fun, ___

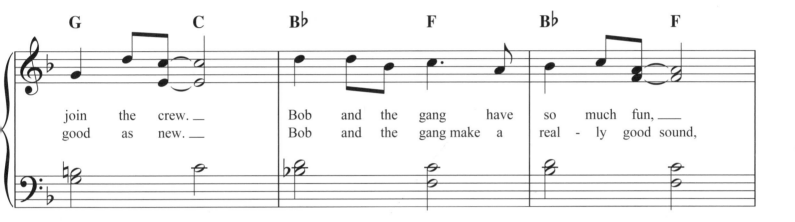

join the crew. ___ Bob and the gang have so much fun, ___
good as new. ___ Bob and the gang make a real - ly good sound,

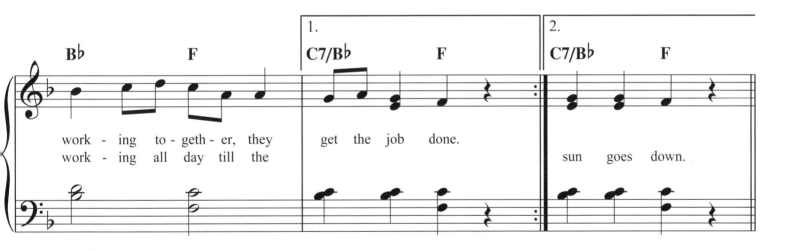

work - ing to - geth - er, they get the job done.
work - ing all day till the sun goes down.

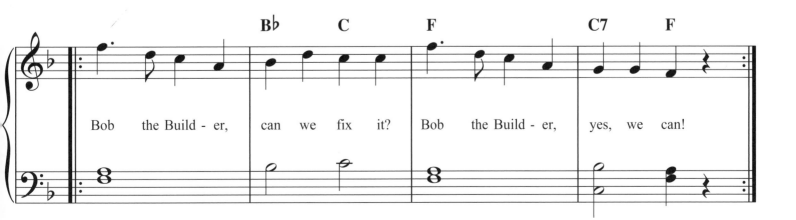

Bob the Build - er, can we fix it? Bob the Build - er, yes, we can!

6

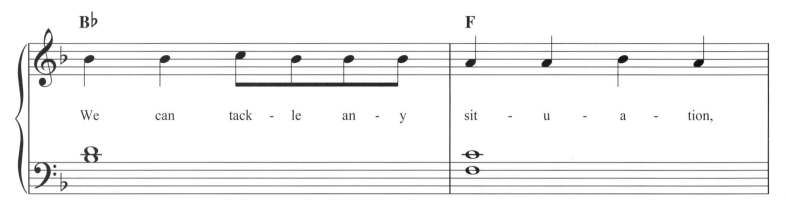

We can tack - le an - y sit - u - a - tion,

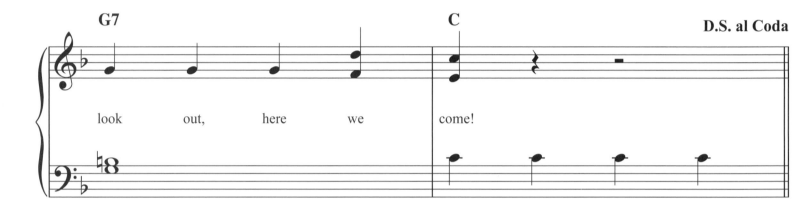

D.S. al Coda

look out, here we come!

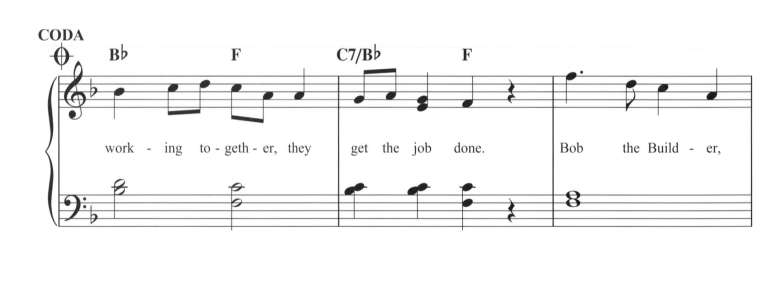

CODA

work - ing to - geth - er, they get the job done. Bob the Build - er,

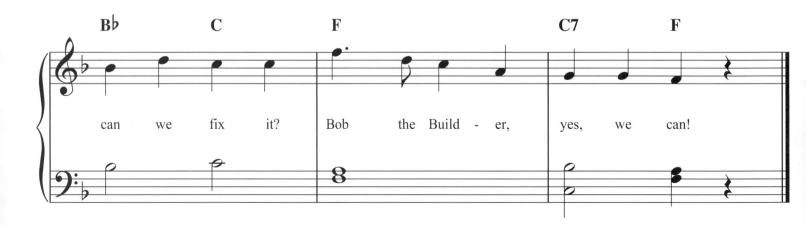

can we fix it? Bob the Build - er, yes, we can!

BATMAN: THE ANIMATED SERIES

(Main Title)

from BATMAN: THE ANIMATED SERIES

By DANNY ELFMAN

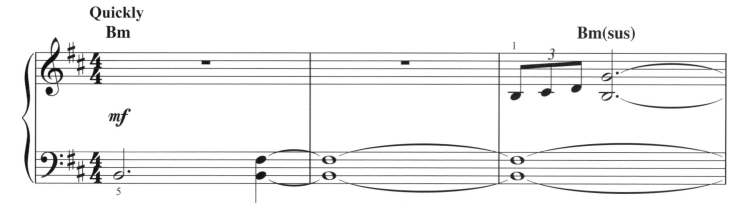

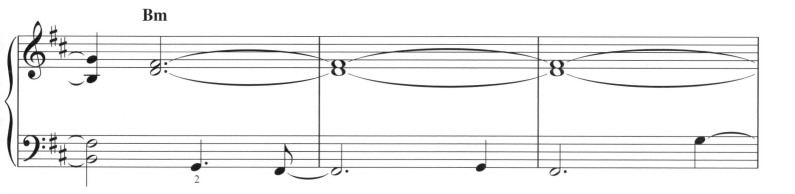

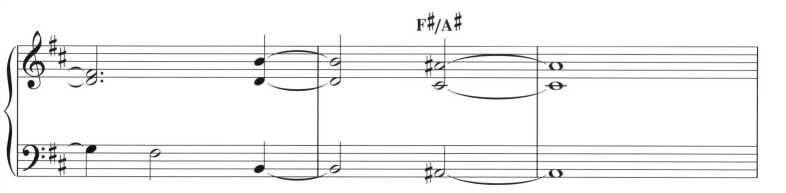

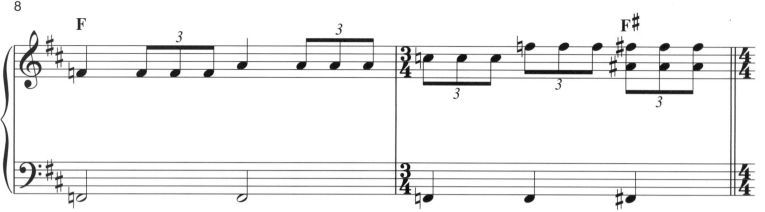

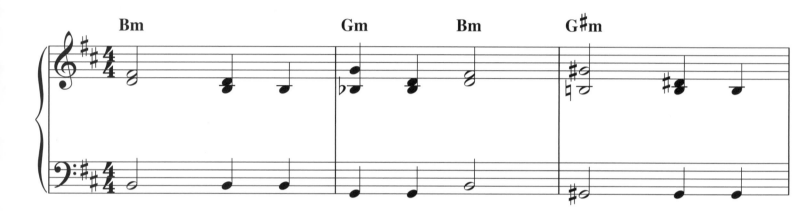

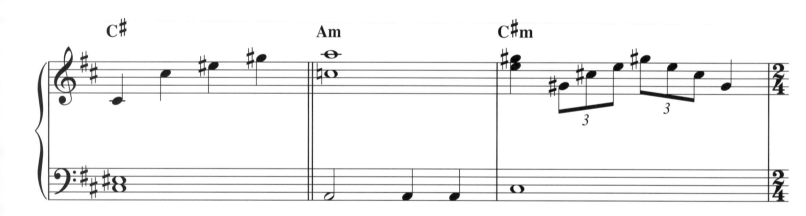

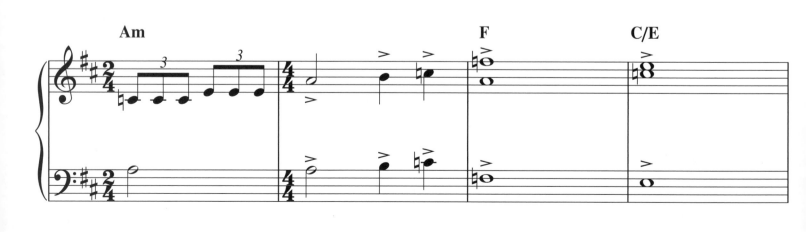

9

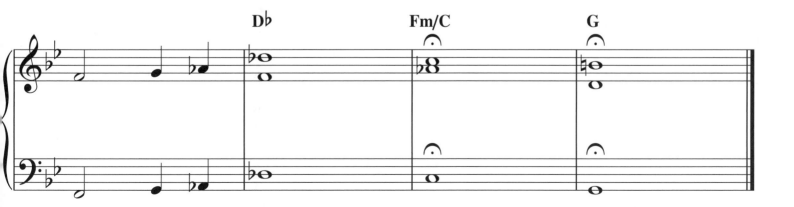

CASPER THE FRIENDLY GHOST

from the Paramount Cartoon

Words by MACK DAVID
Music by JERRY LIVINGSTON

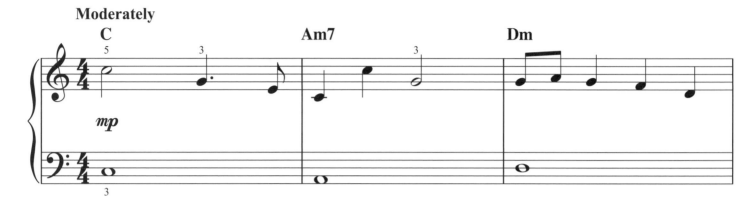

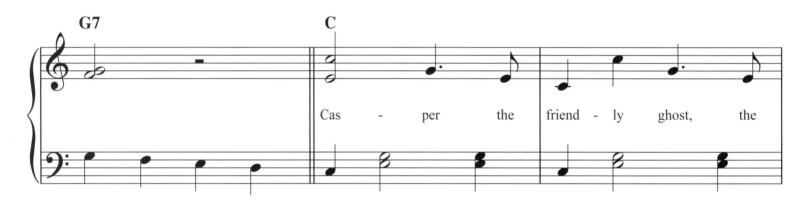

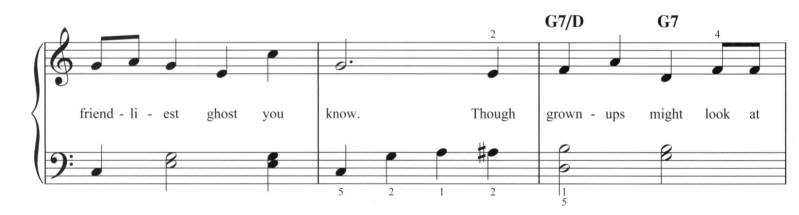

Cas - per the friend - ly ghost, he could-n't be bad or

mean. He'll romp and play, sing and dance all day, the

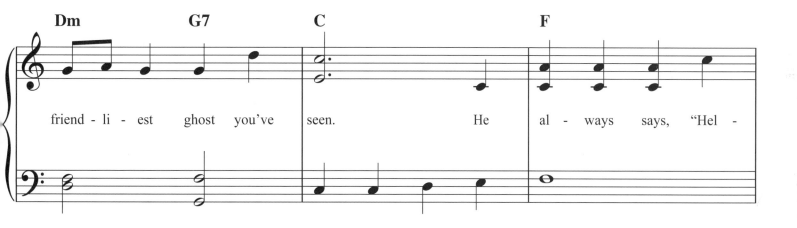

friend - li - est ghost you've seen. He al - ways says, "Hel -

lo," and he's real - ly glad to meet you. Wher -

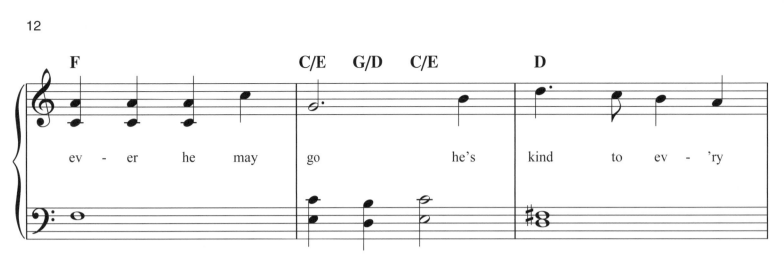

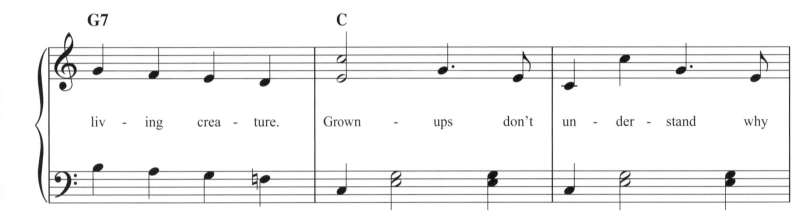

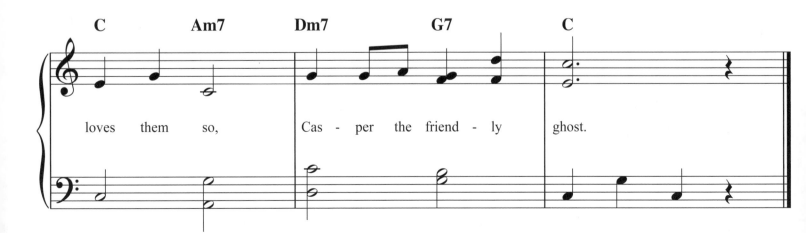

DORA THE EXPLORER THEME SONG

from DORA THE EXPLORER

Words and Music by JOSH SITRON,
SARAH DURKEE and WILLIAM STRAUS

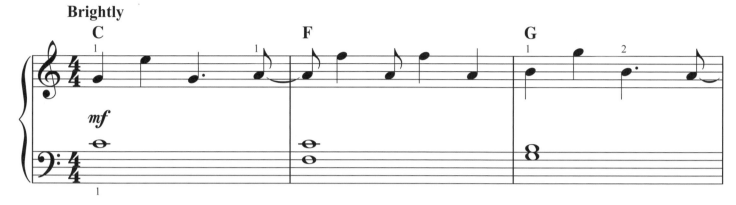

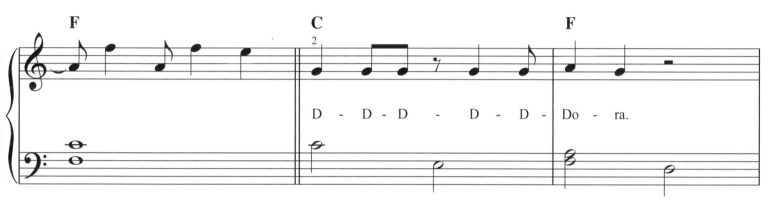

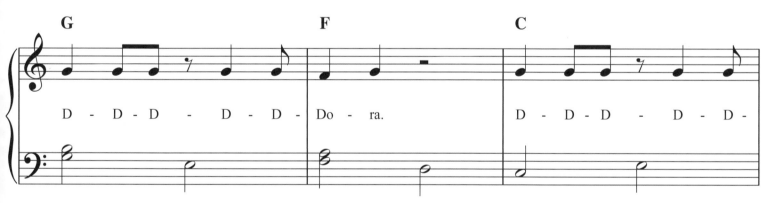

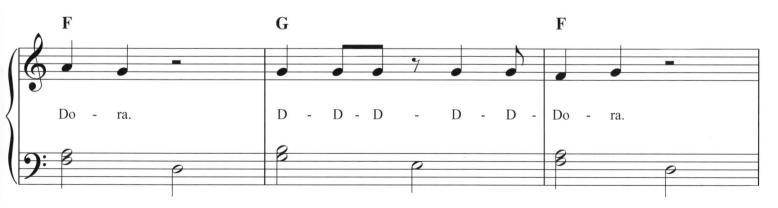

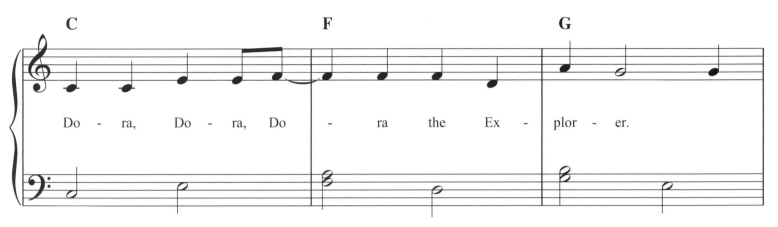

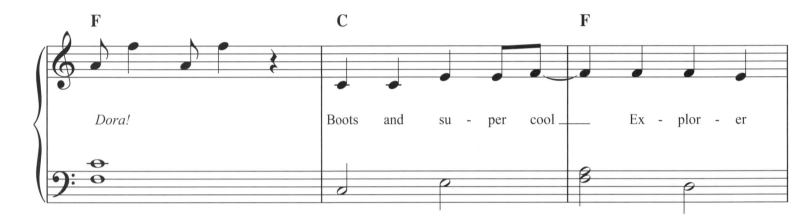

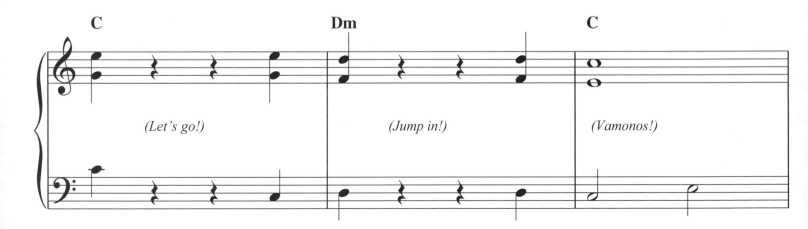

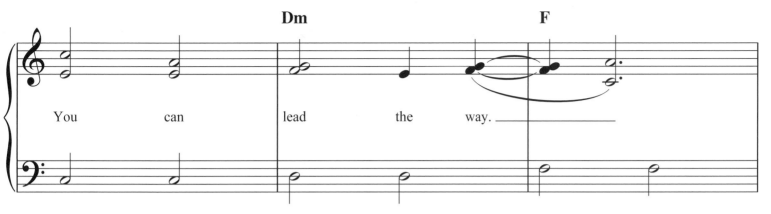

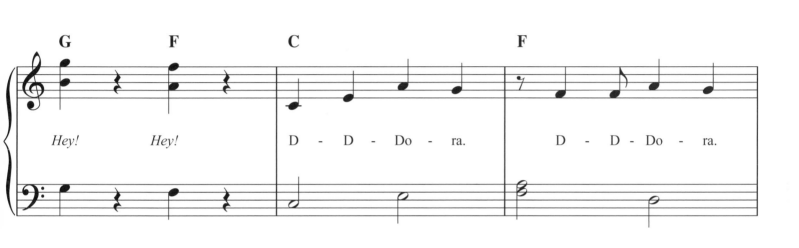

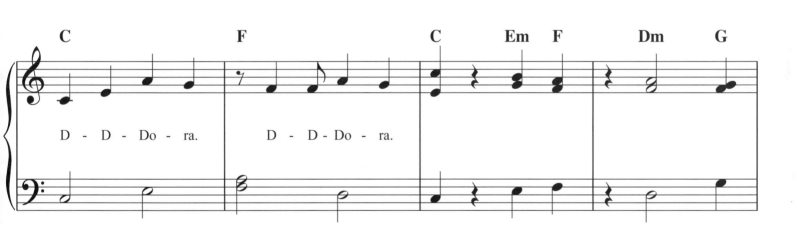

DINOSAUR TRAIN MAIN TITLE

from the Cartoon Series DINOSAUR TRAIN

Written by CRAIG BARTLETT
and JIM LANG

Moderately fast

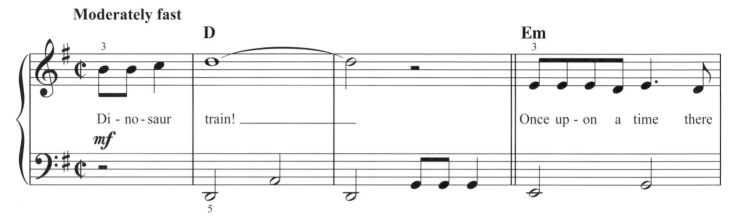

Di - no - saur train! _____ Once up - on a time there

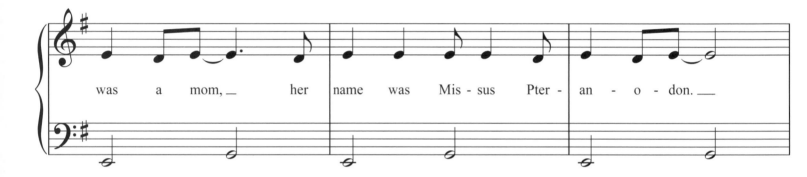

was a mom, ___ her name was Mis - sus Pter - an - o - don. ___

Sit - tin' on her nest, she heard a scratch - ing. She said, "Oh boy! My

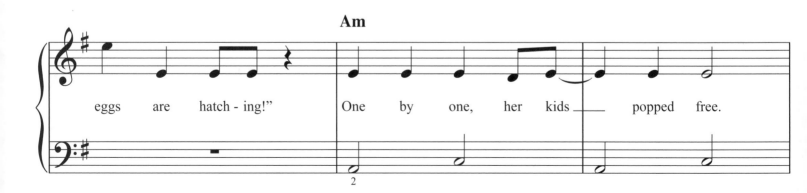

eggs are hatch - ing!" One by one, her kids ___ popped free.

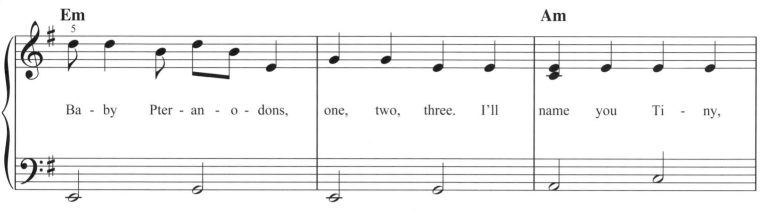

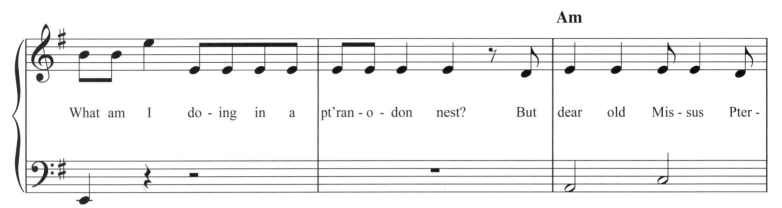

Am

What am I do-ing in a pt'ran-o-don nest? But dear old Mis-sus Pter-

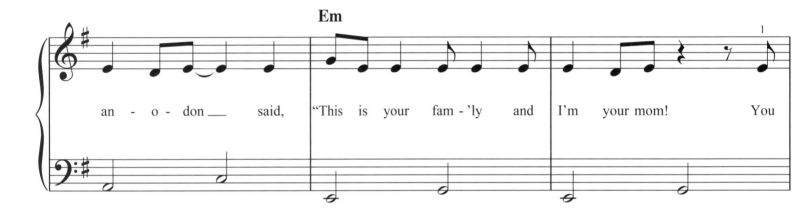

Em

an-o-don __ said, "This is your fam-'ly and I'm your mom! You

Am **B**

may be dif-f'rent, but we're all crea-tures. All di-no-saurs have

Am

dif-f'rent fea-tures." Come on, Bud-dy! We'll take a va-ca-tion! I'll

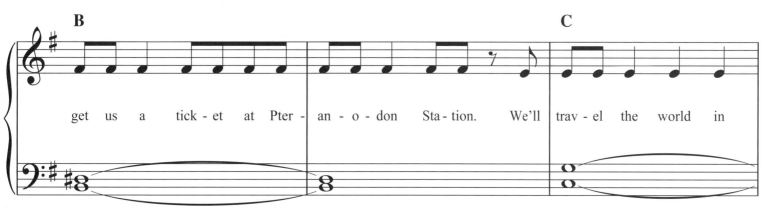

get us a tick - et at Pter - an - o - don Sta - tion. We'll trav - el the world in

sun-shine and rain, and meet all the spe - cies on the Di - no - saur Train! Di - no - saur

Train! Di - no - saur Train! Di - no - saur Train! We're gon - na ride _____

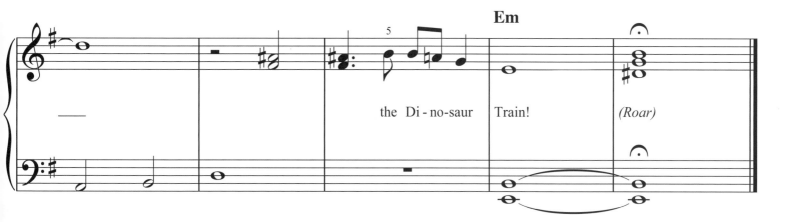

_____ the Di - no - saur Train! (Roar)

DUCKTALES THEME

from THE DISNEY AFTERNOON

Words and Music by
MARK MUELLER

Bright Rock

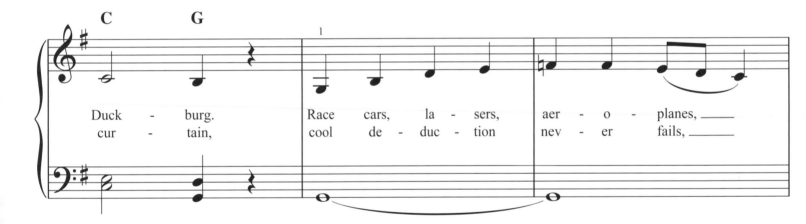

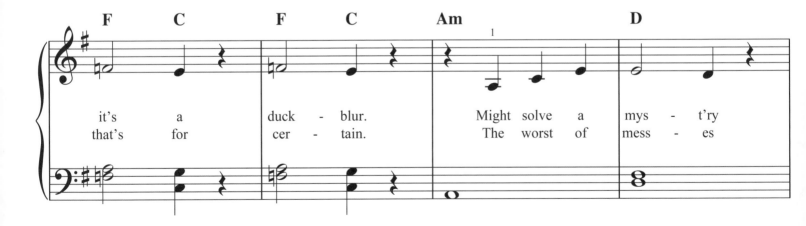

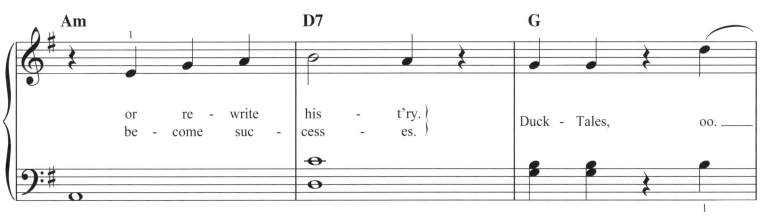

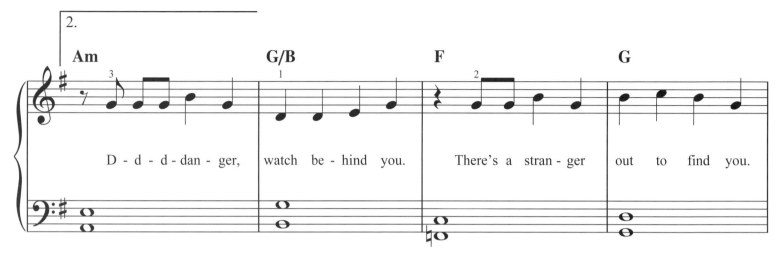

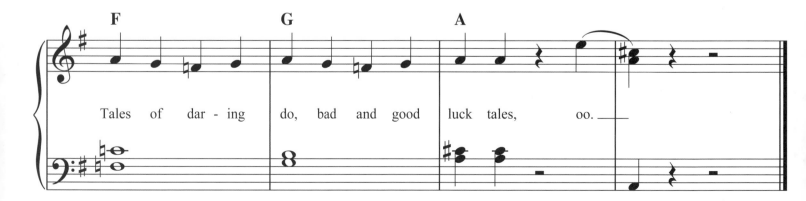

PAW PATROL THEME

Words and Music by JEFF COHEN,
MOLLY KAYE, SCOTT KRIPPAYNE
and MICHAEL "SMIDI" SMITH

Moderately fast

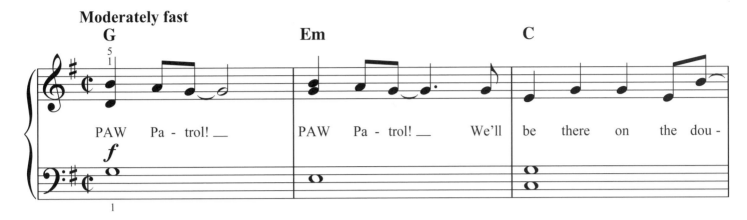

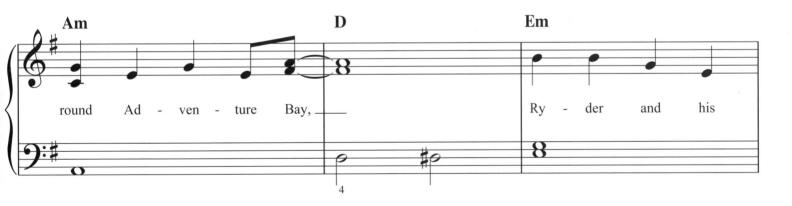

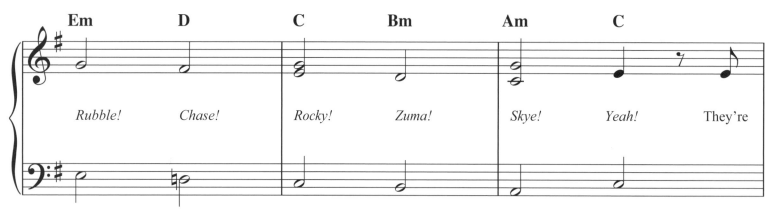

Rubble! Chase! Rocky! Zuma! Skye! Yeah! They're

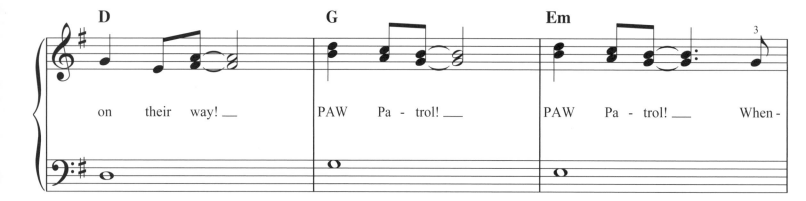

on their way! PAW Pa - trol! PAW Pa - trol! When-

ev - er you're in trou - ble! PAW Pa - trol!

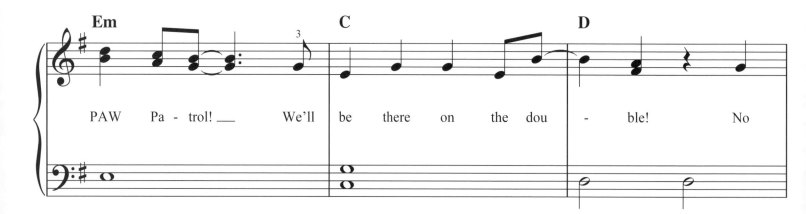

PAW Pa - trol! We'll be there on the dou - ble! No

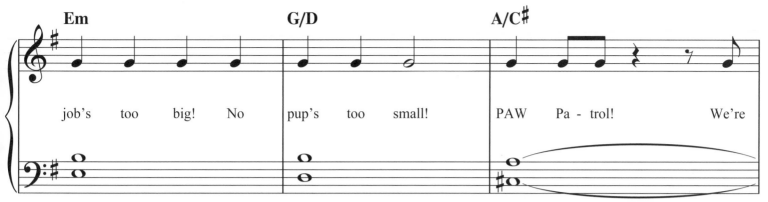

job's too big! No pup's too small! PAW Pa - trol! We're

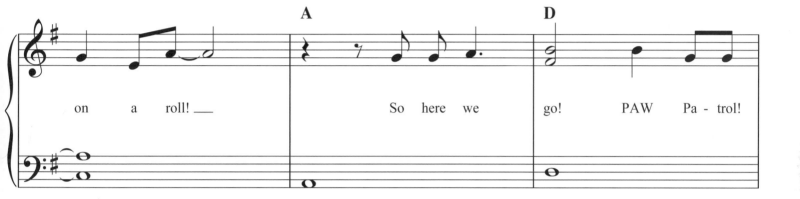

on a roll! ___ So here we go! PAW Pa - trol!

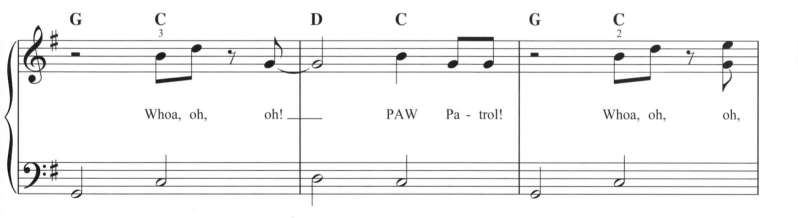

Whoa, oh, oh! ___ PAW Pa - trol! Whoa, oh, oh,

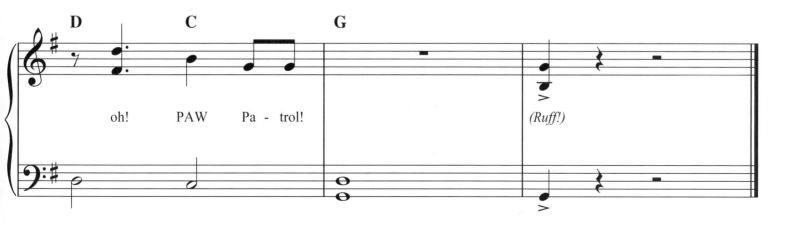

oh! PAW Pa - trol! *(Ruff!)*

I'M POPEYE THE SAILOR MAN

Theme from the Paramount Cartoon POPEYE THE SAILOR

Words and Music by
SAMMY LERNER

Moderately

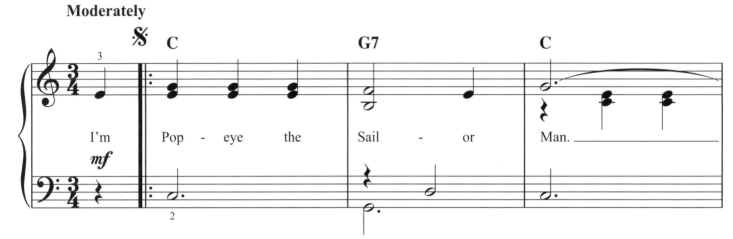

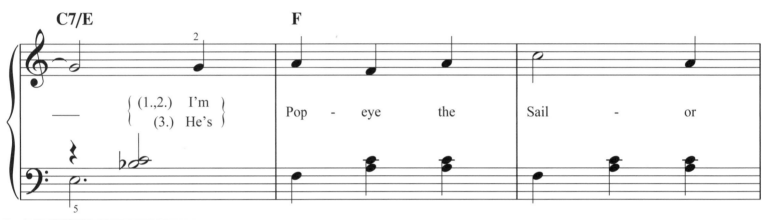

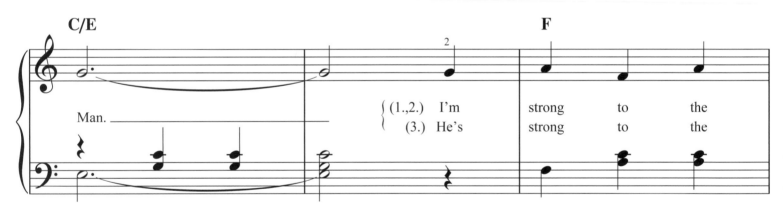

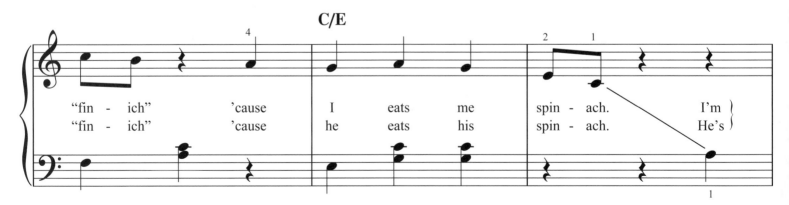

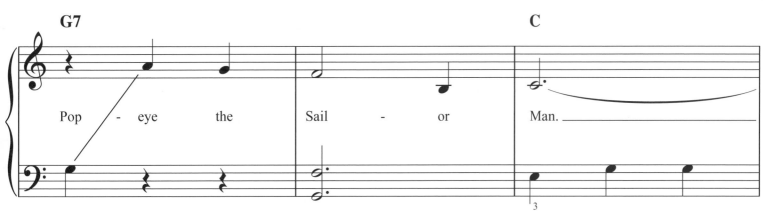

Pop - eye the Sail - or Man. _____

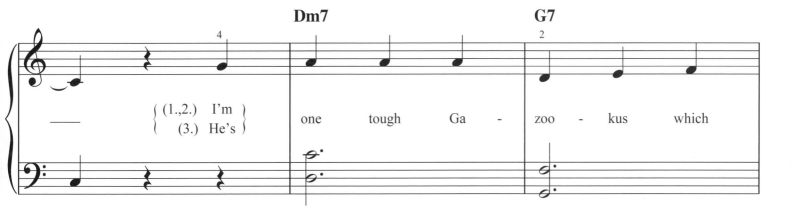

_____ { (1.,2.) I'm / (3.) He's } one tough Ga - zoo - kus which

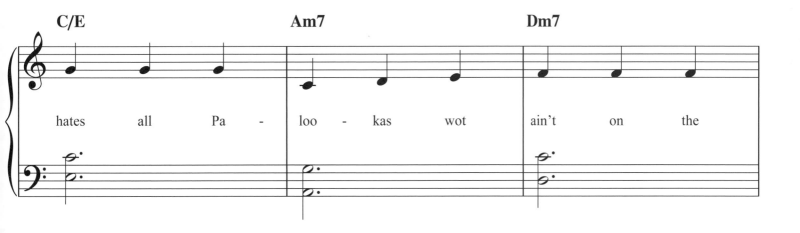

hates all Pa - loo - kas wot ain't on the

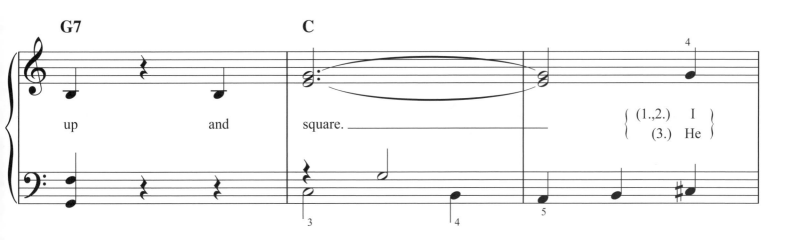

up and square. _____ { (1.,2.) I / (3.) He }

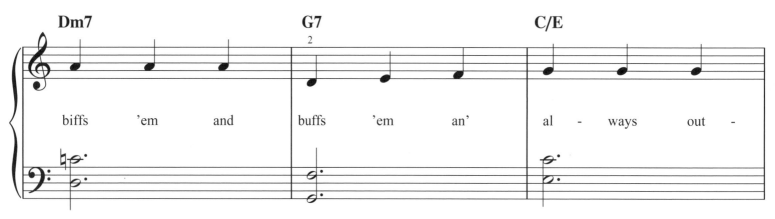

Dm7   **G7**   **C/E**

biffs   'em   and   buffs   'em   an'   al - ways   out -

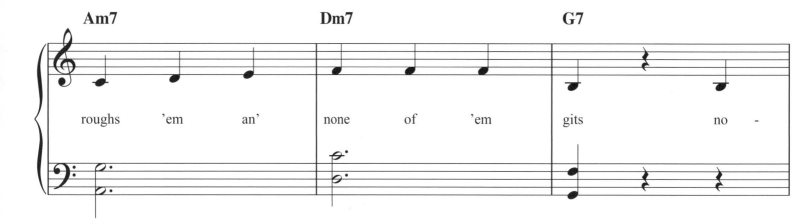

Am7   **Dm7**   **G7**

roughs   'em   an'   none   of   'em   gits   no -

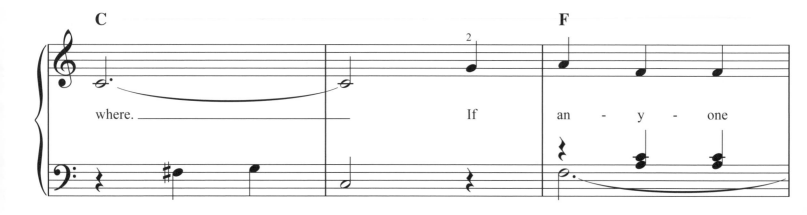

C   **F**

where. _____   If   an - y - one

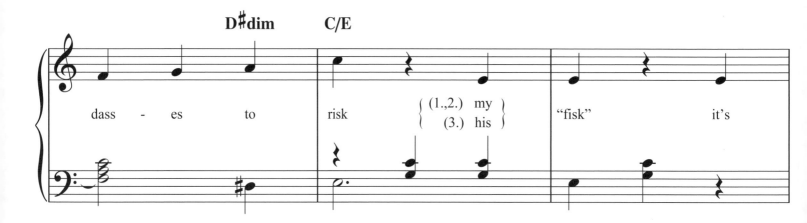

                  D♯dim   **C/E**

dass - es   to   risk   { (1.,2.) my / (3.) his }   "fisk"   it's

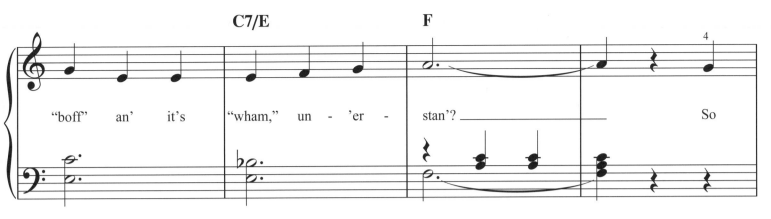

"boff" an' it's "wham," un - 'er - stan'? _____ So

keep "good be - hav - 'or," that's your one life - sav - er with

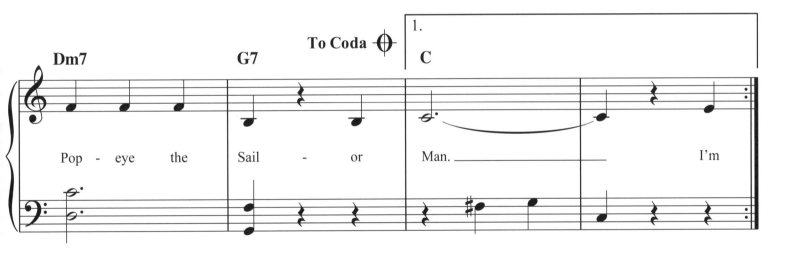

Pop - eye the Sail - or Man. _____ I'm

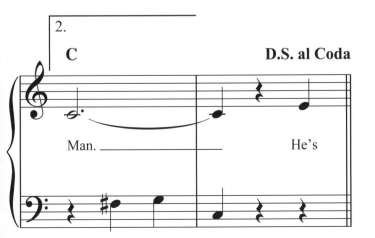

2. C — D.S. al Coda — Man. _____ He's

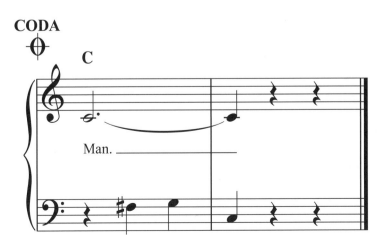

CODA C — Man. _____

LINUS AND LUCY
from A CHARLIE BROWN CHRISTMAS

By VINCE GUARALDI

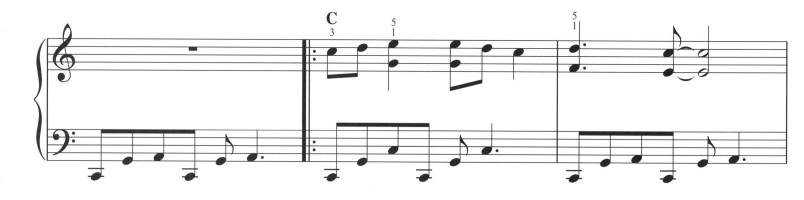

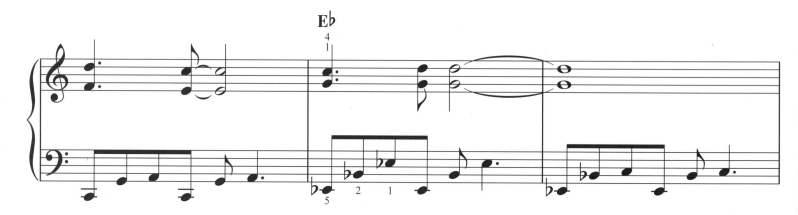

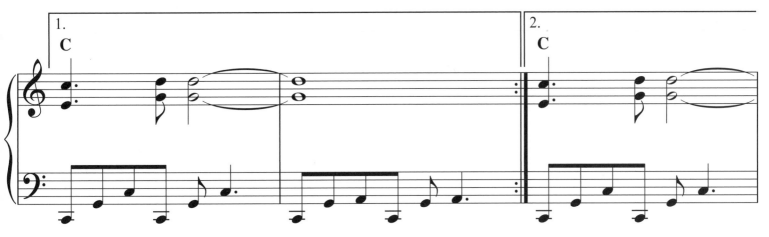

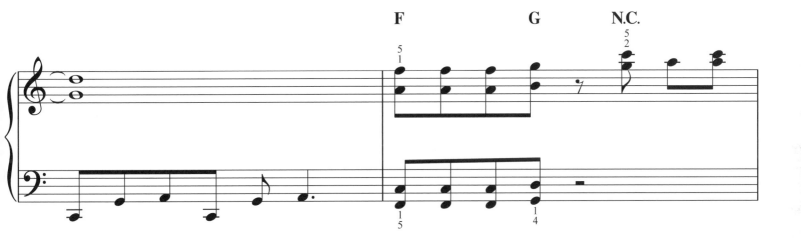

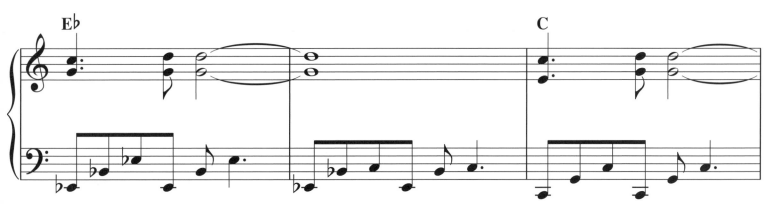

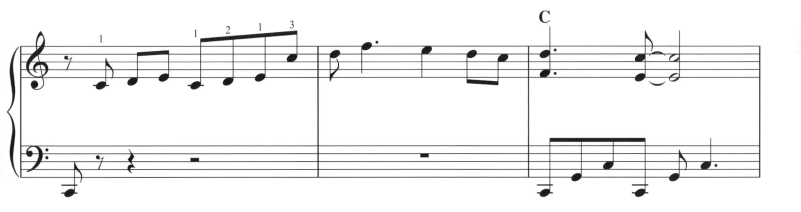

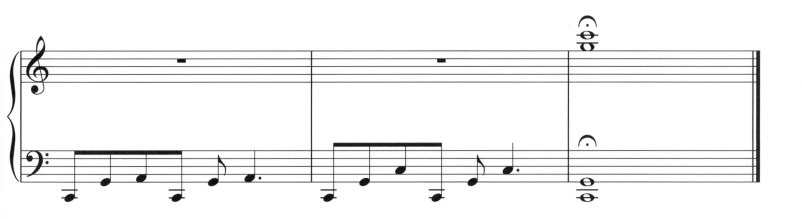

MICKEY MOUSE MARCH

from THE MICKEY MOUSE CLUB

Words and Music by
JIMMIE DODD

Brightly

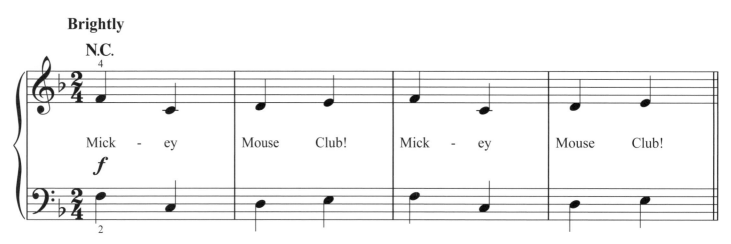

Mick - ey   Mouse Club!   Mick - ey   Mouse Club!

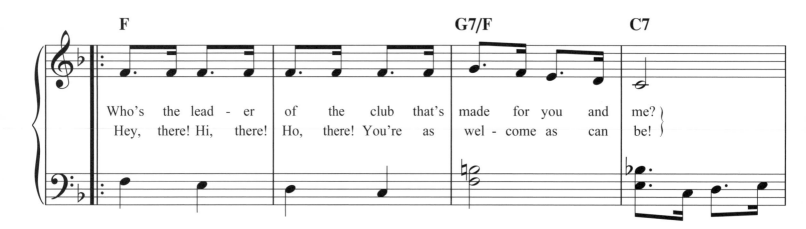

Who's the lead - er   of the club that's   made for you and   me?
Hey, there! Hi, there!   Ho, there! You're as   wel - come as can   be!

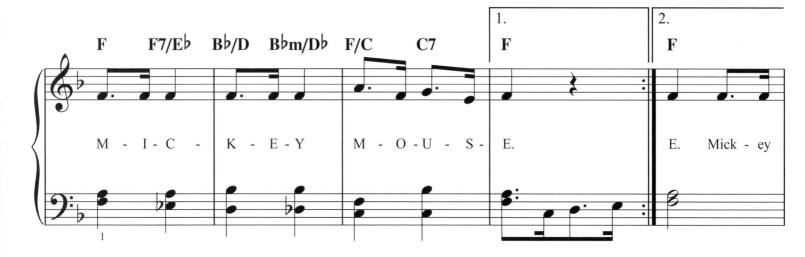

M - I - C - K - E - Y   M - O - U - S - E.   E. Mick - ey

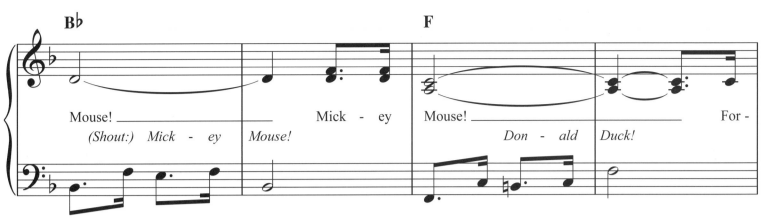

Mouse! _____ Mick - ey Mouse! _____ For -
(Shout:) Mick - ey Mouse! Don - ald Duck!

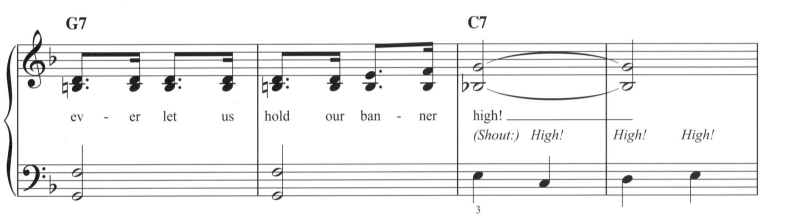

ev - er let us hold our ban - ner high! _____
(Shout:) High! High! High!

Come a - long and sing a song and join our jam - bor - ee!

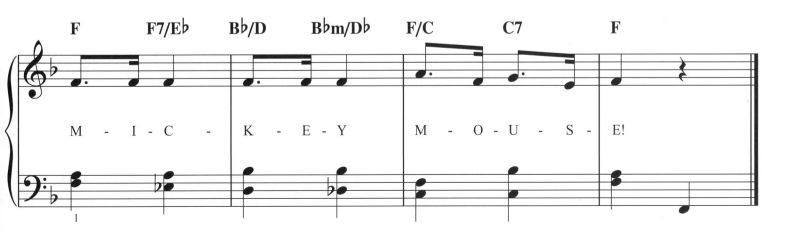

M - I - C - K - E - Y M - O - U - S - E!

OCTONAUTS MAIN TITLE

Words and Music by
DARREN HENDLEY

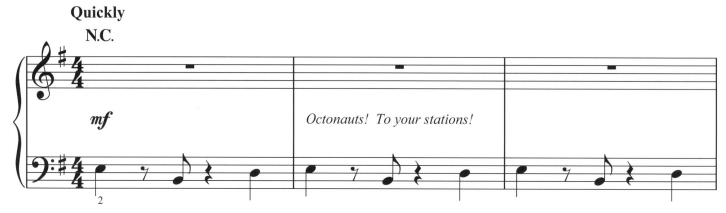

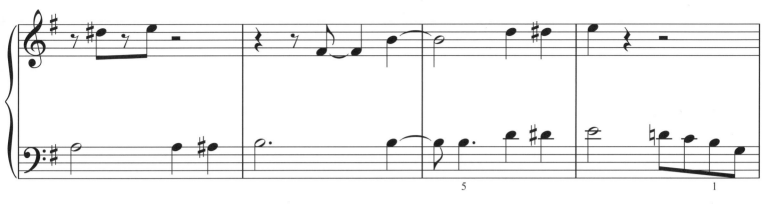

Explore!

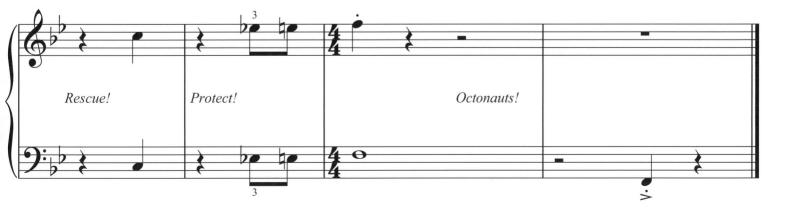

Rescue!   *Protect!*   *Octonauts!*

PJ MASKS

Words and Music by ERIC RENWART
and DAVID FREEDMAN

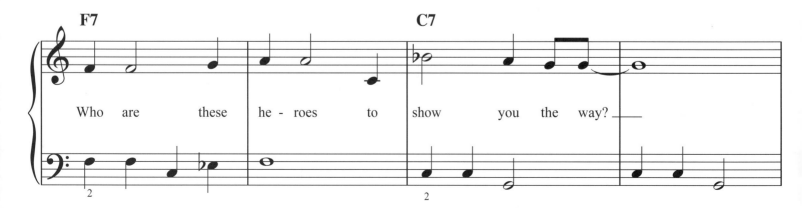

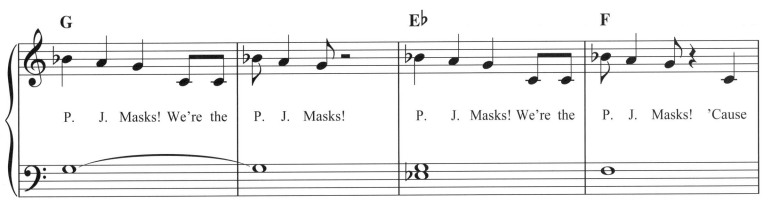

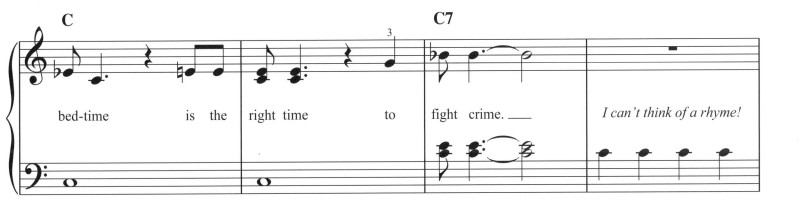

POKÉMON THEME
Theme to the English adapted anime series POKÉMON

Words and Music by T. LOEFFLER
and J. SIEGLER

Moderately fast, with a driving beat

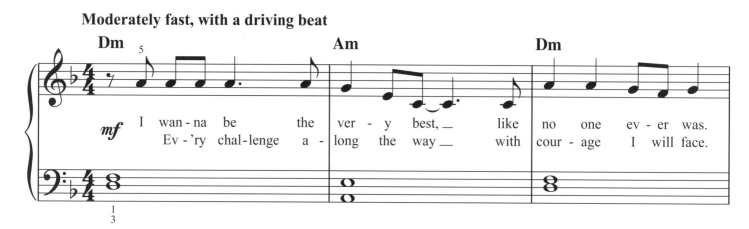

I wan-na be the ver-y best, __ like no one ev-er was.
Ev-'ry chal-lenge a-long the way __ with cour-age I will face.

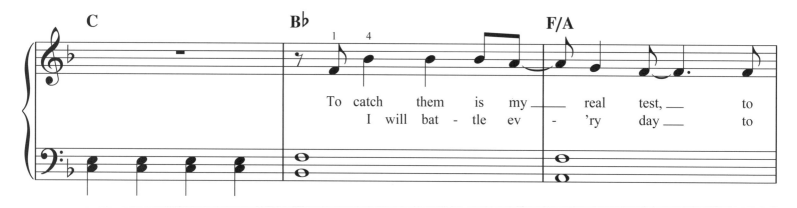

To catch them is my __ real test, __ to
I will bat-tle ev-'ry day __ to

train them is __ my cause. __
claim my right-ful place. __

I will trav-el a-
Come with me; the

cross the land, __ search-ing far and wide, __
time is right. __ There's no bet-ter team.

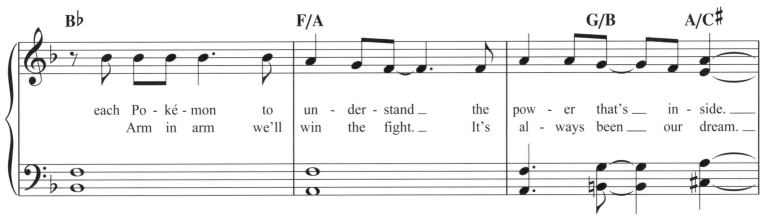

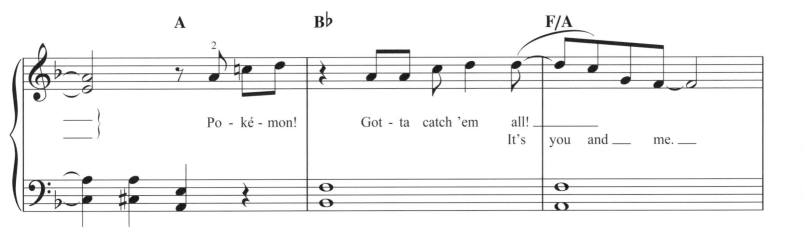

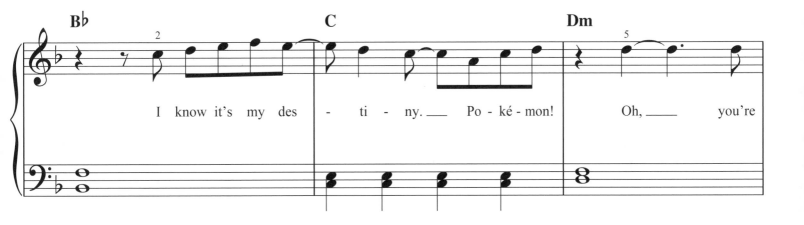

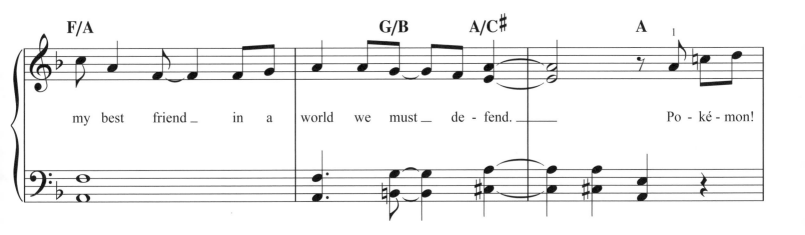

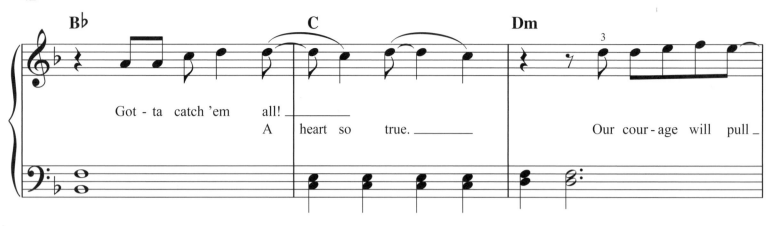

Got - ta catch 'em all! ____
A heart so true. ____
Our cour - age will pull

____ us through. _ You teach me ____ and I'll ____ teach you. ____

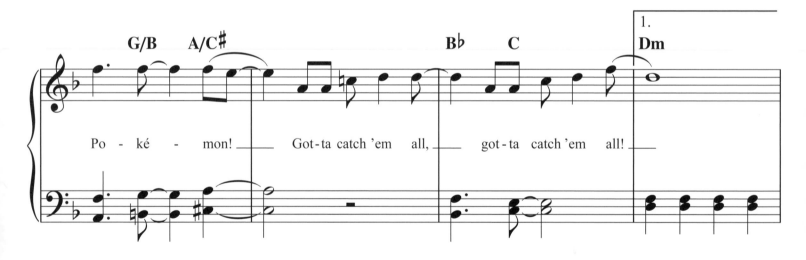

Po - ké - mon! ____ Got - ta catch 'em all, ____ got - ta catch 'em all! ____

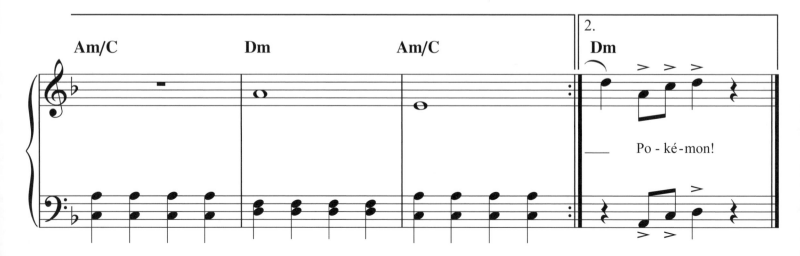

____ Po - ké - mon!

ROCKY & BULLWINKLE
from the Cartoon Television Series

Words and Music by
FRANK G. COMSTOCK

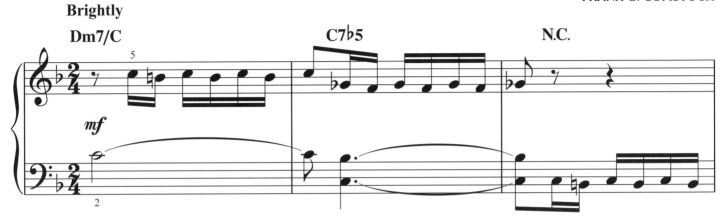

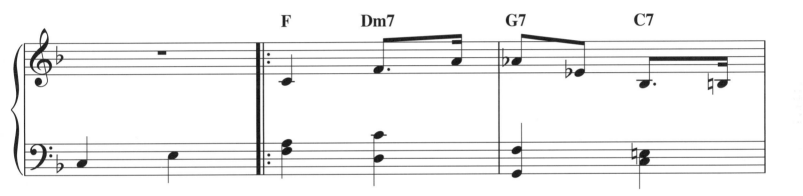

44

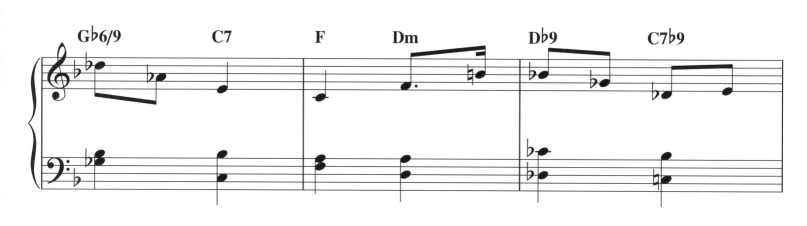

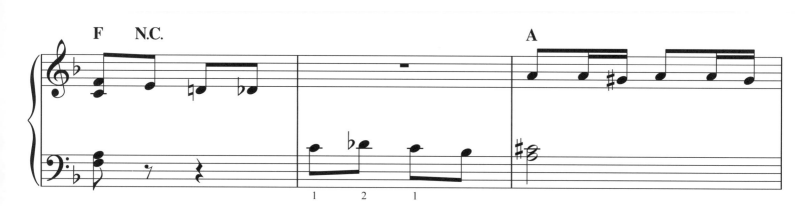

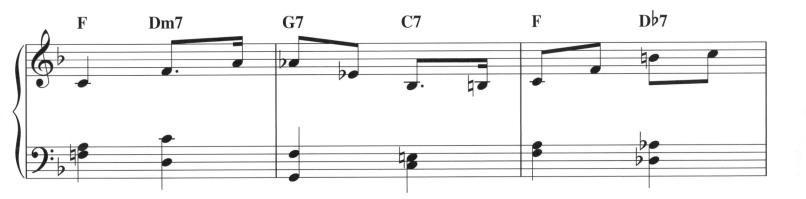

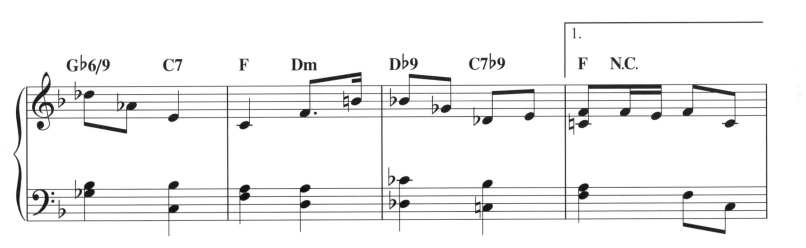

RUGRATS THEME (T.V.)

Words and Music by
MARK MOTHERSBAUGH

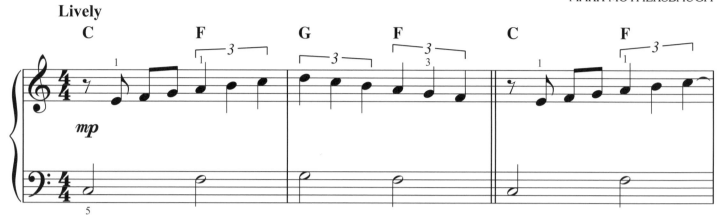

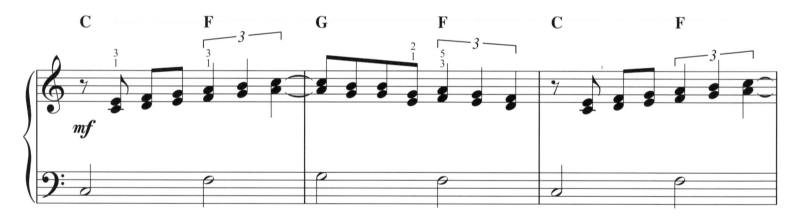

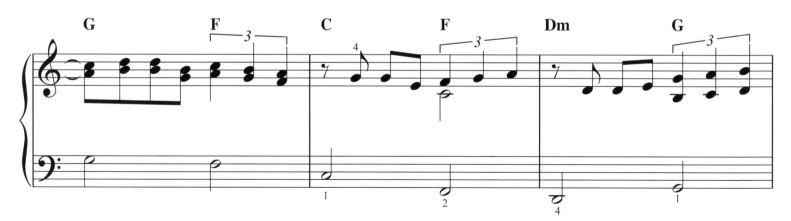

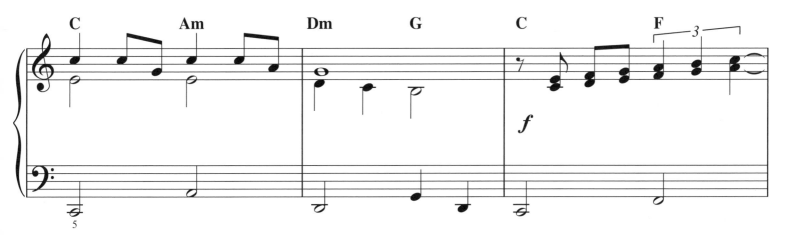

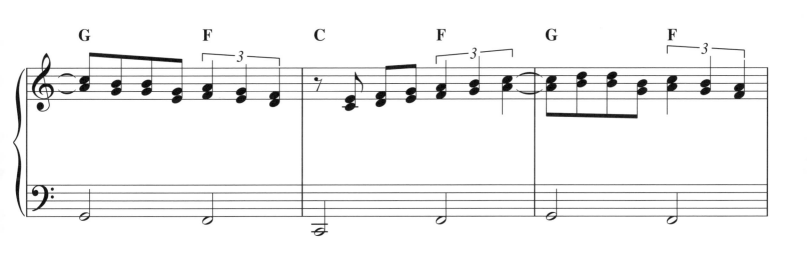

THEME FROM SPIDER MAN

Written by BOB HARRIS
and PAUL FRANCIS WEBSTER

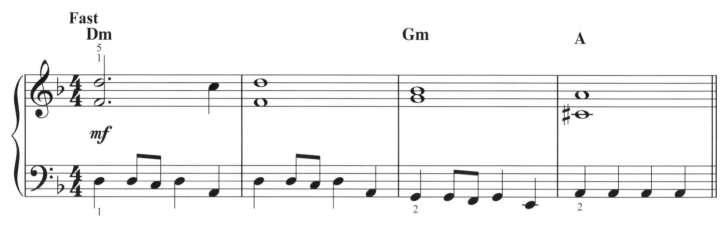

1.

Dm　　**Dm6**

Here comes the Spi - der Man.
There goes the Spi - der

2.

Dm　　　　　　　　　　**C**　　　　　　**F**　**Gm/B♭**

Man.　　　*mp*　In the chill of night,＿ at the

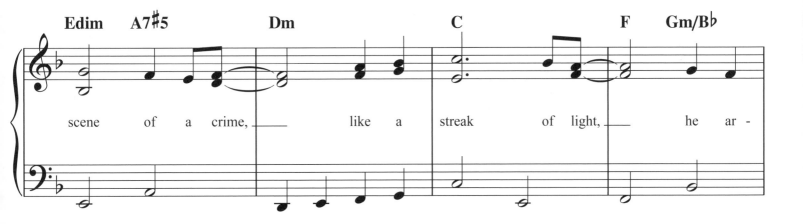

Edim　　**A7#5**　　　　**Dm**　　　　　**C**　　　　　**F**　**Gm/B♭**

scene of a crime,＿ like a streak of light,＿ he ar -

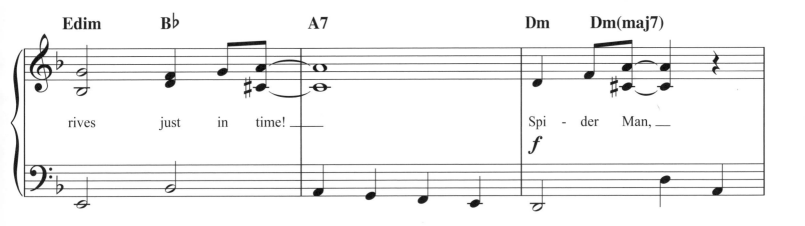

Edim　　　　**B♭**　　　　　　**A7**　　　　　　**Dm**　　**Dm(maj7)**

rives just in time! ＿ Spi - der Man,＿

f

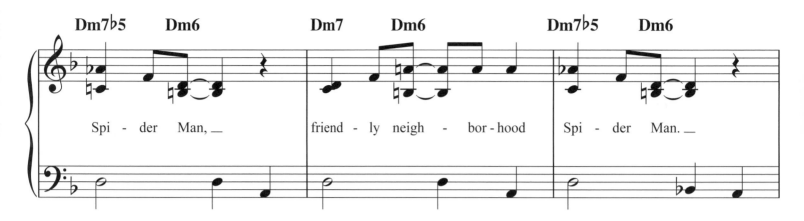

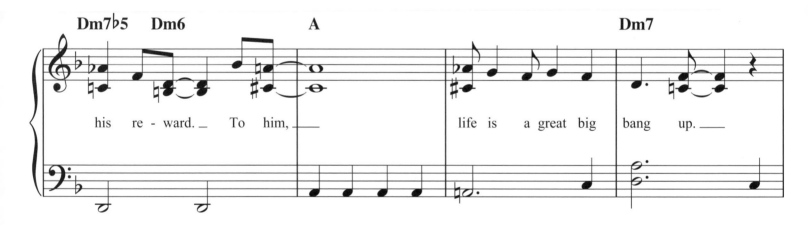

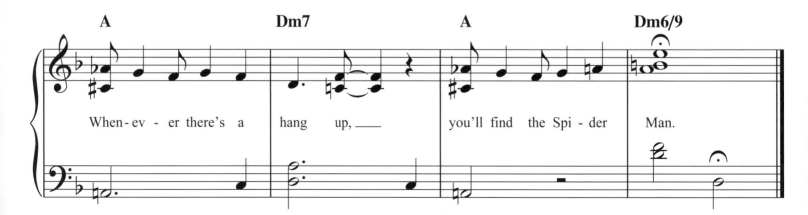

THEME FROM THE SIMPSONS™

from the Twentieth Century Fox Television Series THE SIMPSONS

Music by
DANNY ELFMAN

Moderately fast, in 2

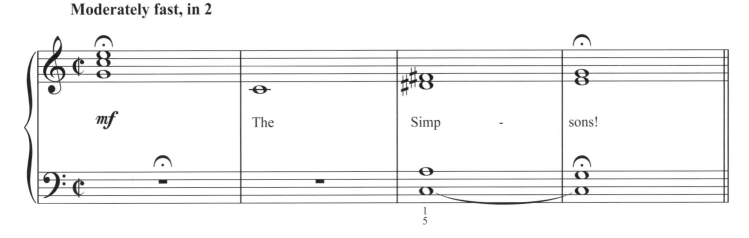

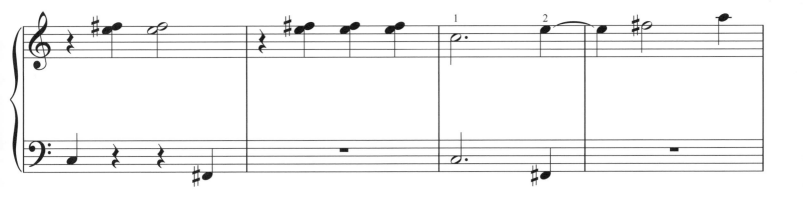

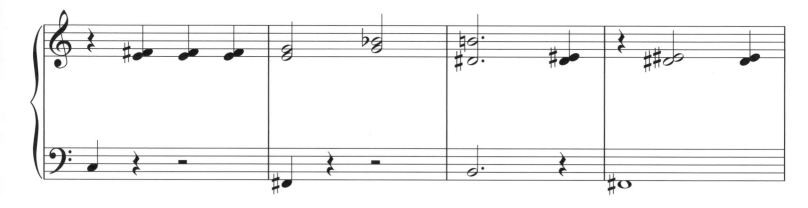

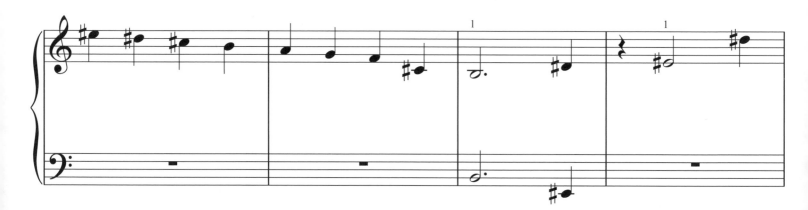

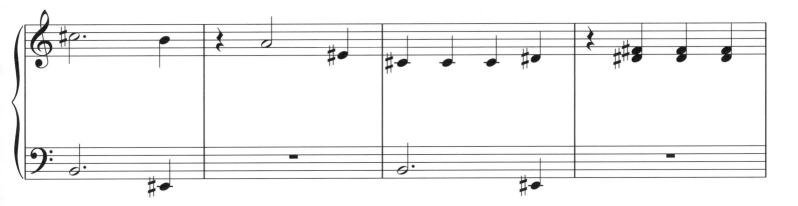

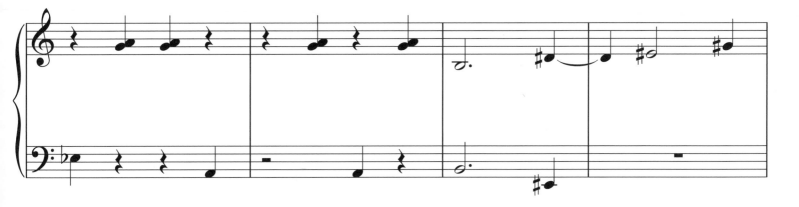

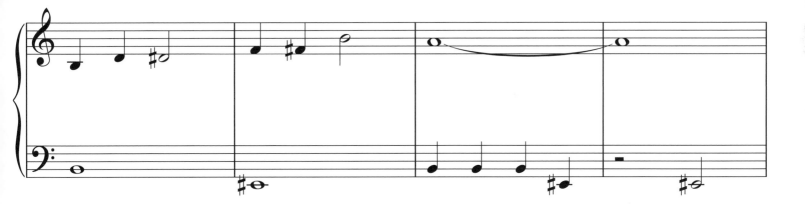

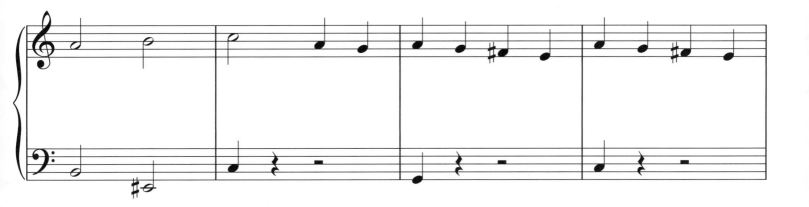

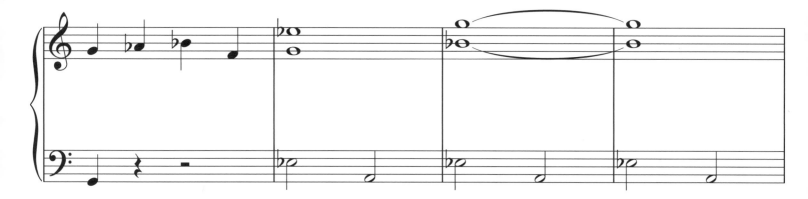

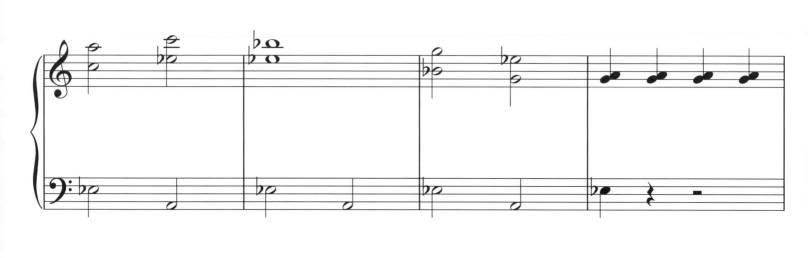

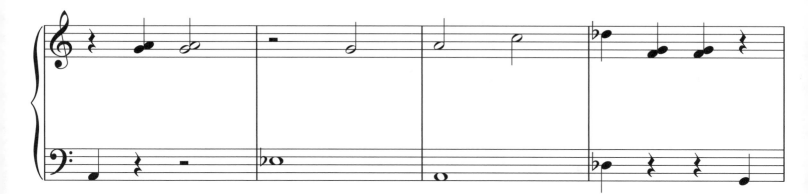

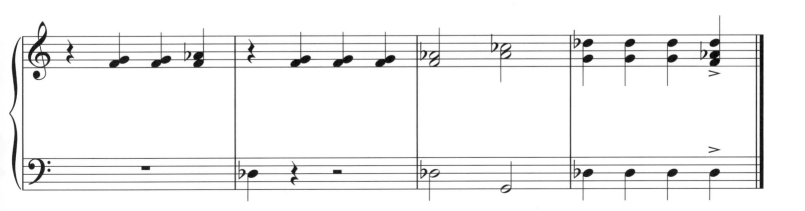

SOFIA THE FIRST MAIN TITLE THEME

from SOFIA THE FIRST

Written by JOHN KAVANAUGH
and CRAIG GERBER

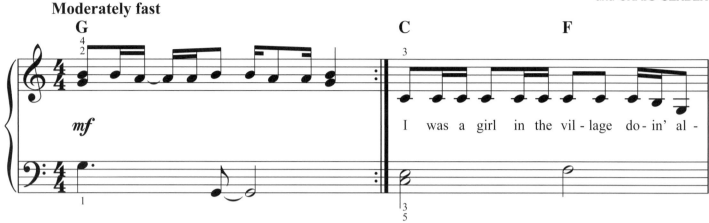

I was a girl in the vil-lage do-in' al-

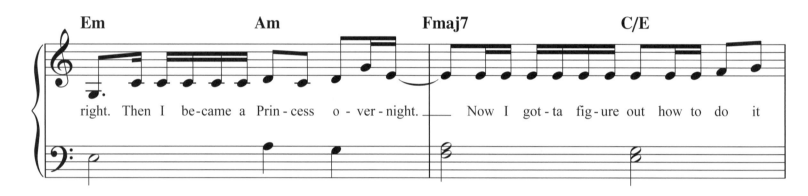

right. Then I be-came a Prin-cess o-ver-night. Now I got-ta fig-ure out how to do it

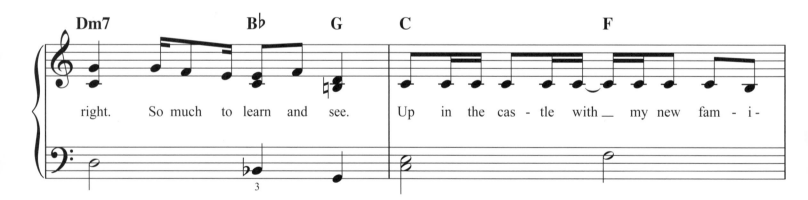

right. So much to learn and see. Up in the cas-tle with __ my new fam-i-

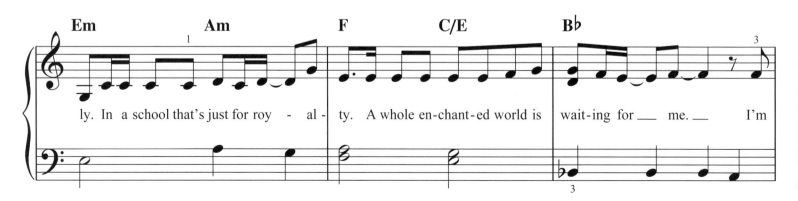

ly. In a school that's just for roy - al-ty. A whole en-chant-ed world is wait-ing for __ me. I'm

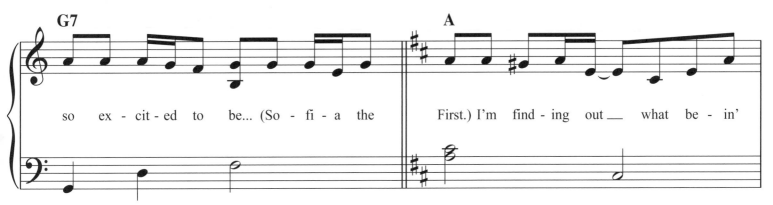

so ex - cit - ed to be... (So - fi - a the First.) I'm find - ing out ___ what be - in'

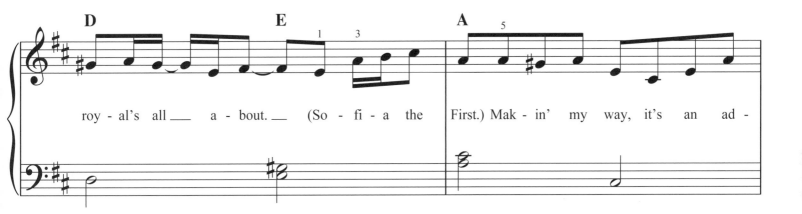

roy - al's all ___ a - bout. ___ (So - fi - a the First.) Mak - in' my way, it's an ad -

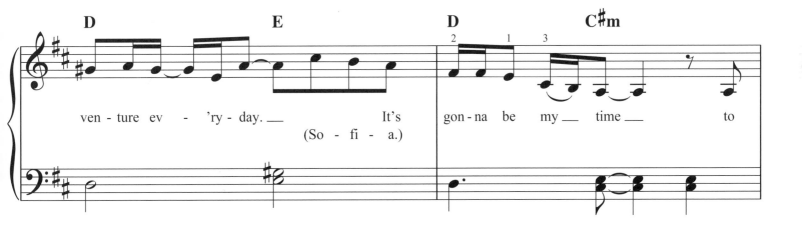

ven - ture ev - 'ry - day. ___ It's gon - na be my ___ time ___ to
(So - fi - a.)

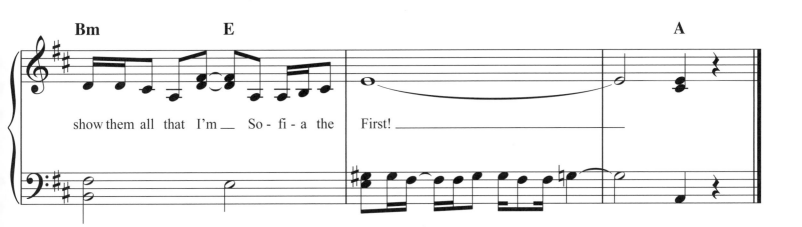

show them all that I'm ___ So - fi - a the First! _____

SPONGEBOB SQUAREPANTS THEME SONG

from SPONGEBOB SQUAREPANTS

Words and Music by MARK HARRISON,
BLAISE SMITH, STEVE HILLENBURG
and DEREK DRYMON

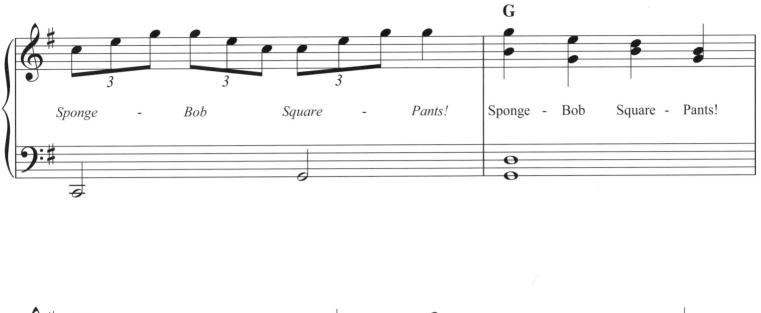

Sponge - Bob Square - Pants! | Sponge - Bob Square - Pants!

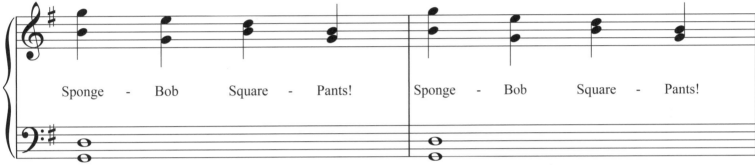

Sponge - Bob Square - Pants! | Sponge - Bob Square - Pants!

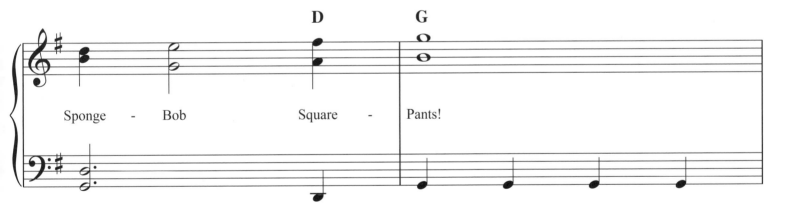

Sponge - Bob Square - Pants!

TEAM UMIZUMI THEME

Words and Music by MARY HAYE,
PT WALKLEY and SCOTT HOLLINGSWORTH

With energy

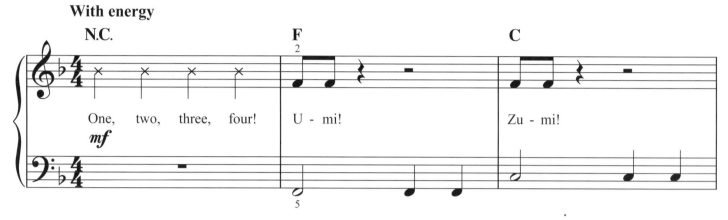

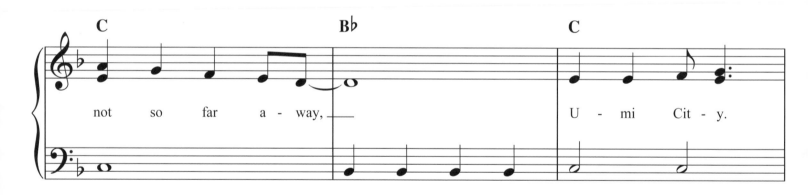

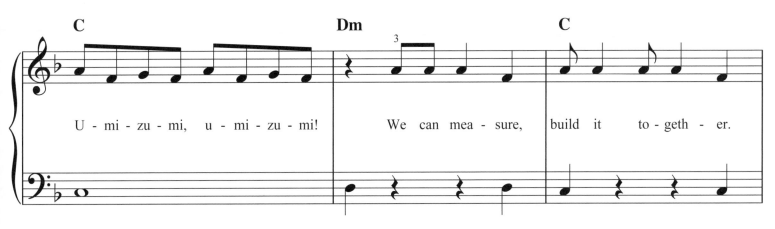

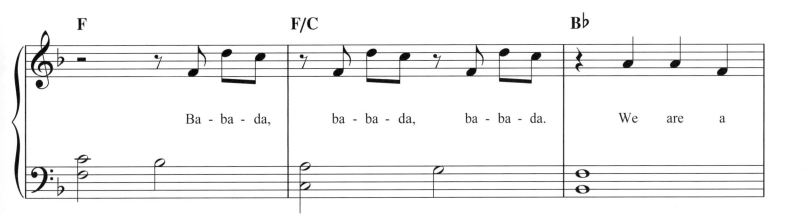

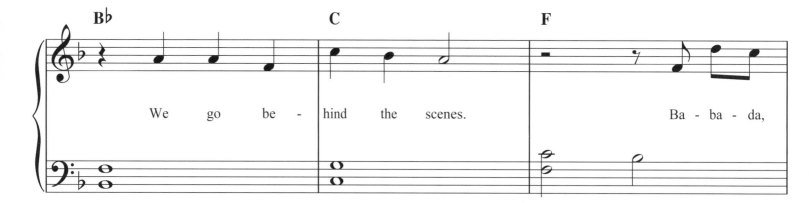

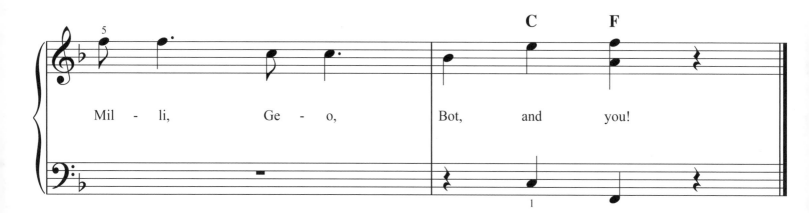

THOMAS THE TANK ENGINE
(Main Title)
from THOMAS THE TANK ENGINE

Words and Music by
ED WELCH

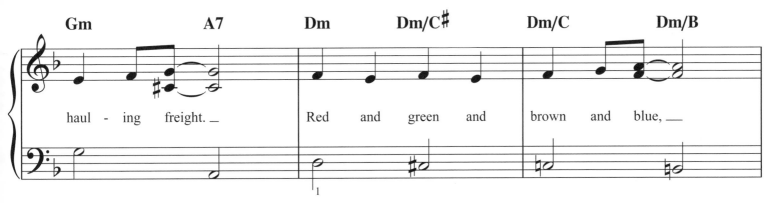

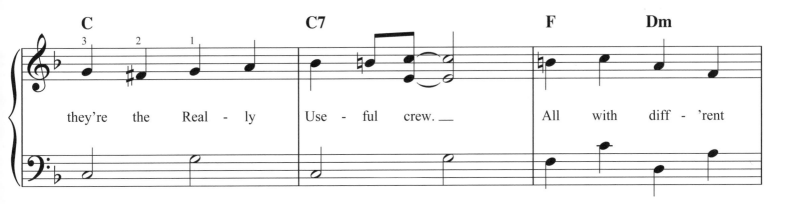

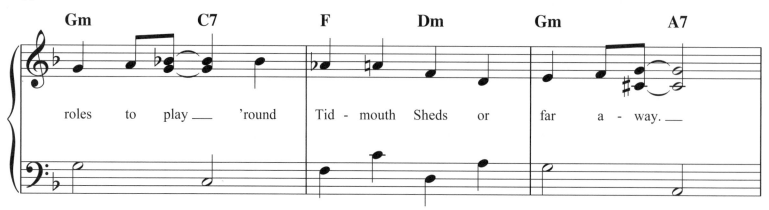

roles to play ___ 'round | Tid - mouth Sheds or | far a - way. ___

Down the hills and | 'round the bends, _ | Thom - as and his | friends.

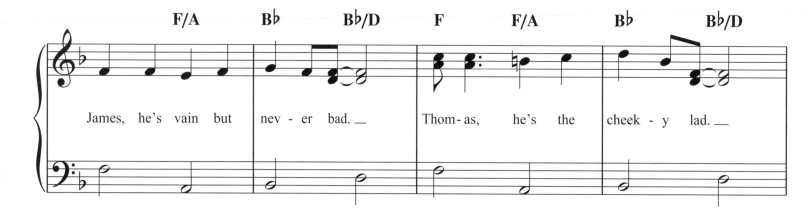

James, he's vain but | nev - er bad. _ | Thom - as, he's the | cheek - y lad. _

Per - cy hauls the | mail on time. _ | Gor - don thun - ders | down the line. _

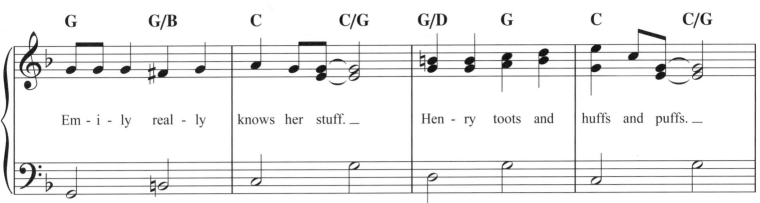

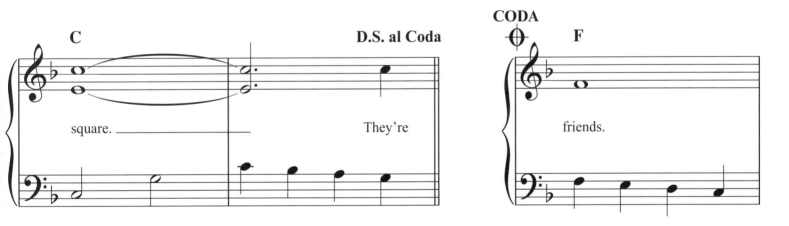

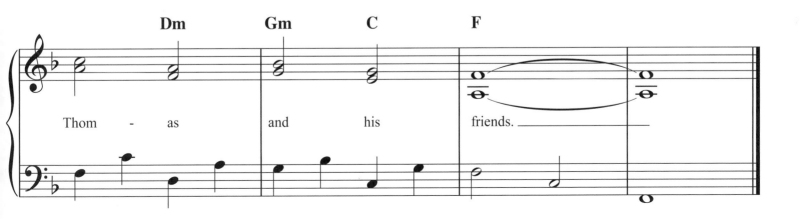

THIS IS IT!
Theme from THE BUGS BUNNY SHOW

Words and Music by MACK DAVID
and JERRY LIVINGSTON

Bright Showtune tempo

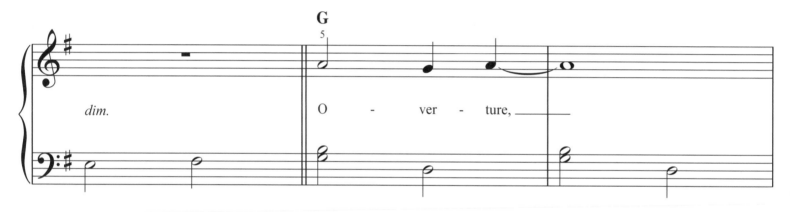

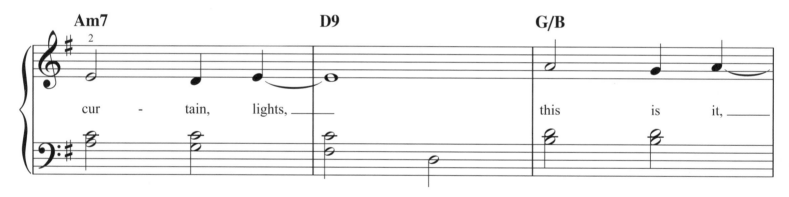

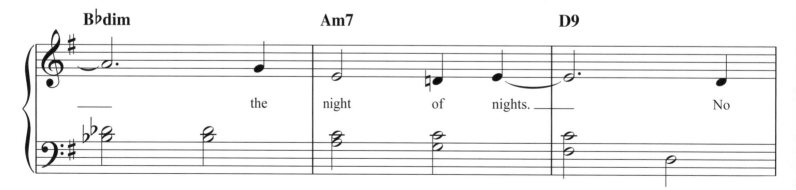

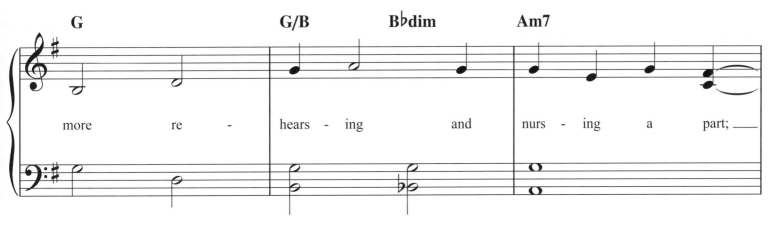

more re - hears - ing and nurs - ing a part; ____

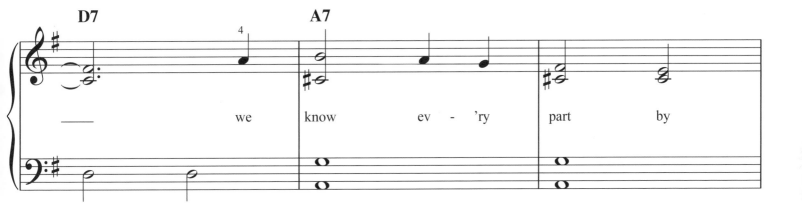

____ we know ev - 'ry part by

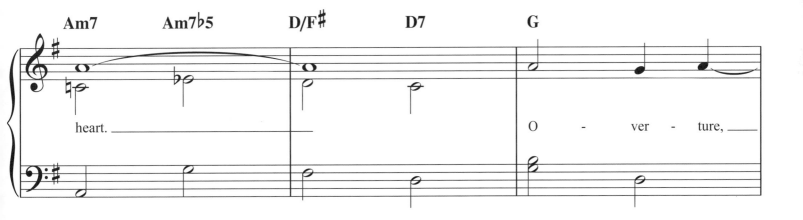

heart. ____ O - ver - ture, ____

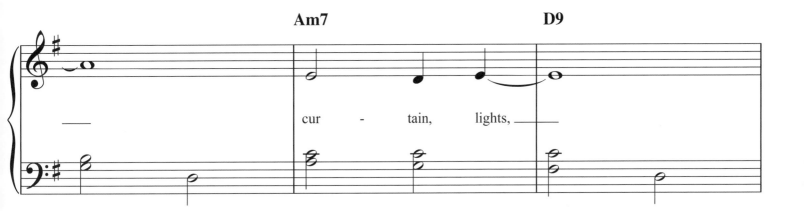

cur - tain, lights, ____

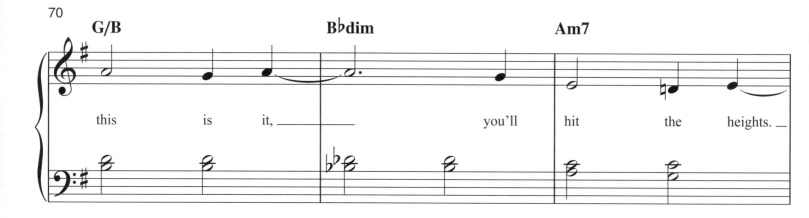

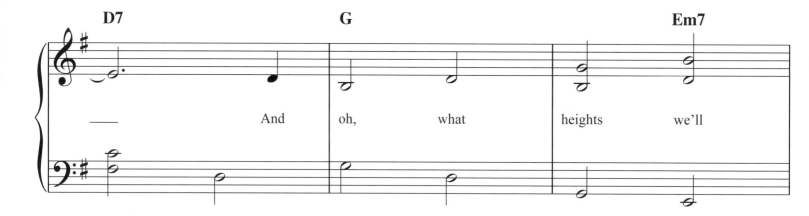

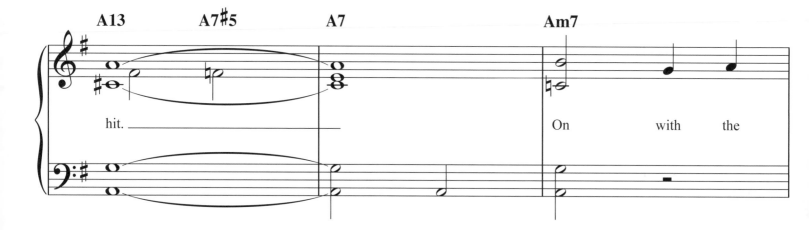

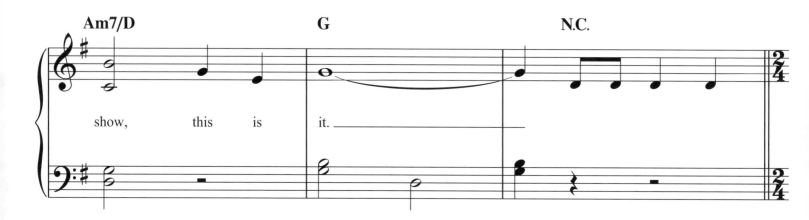

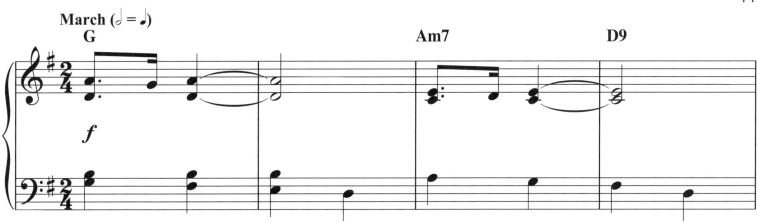

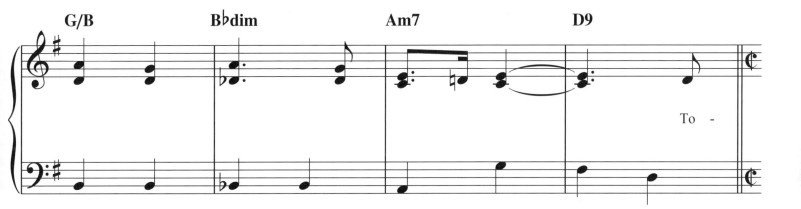

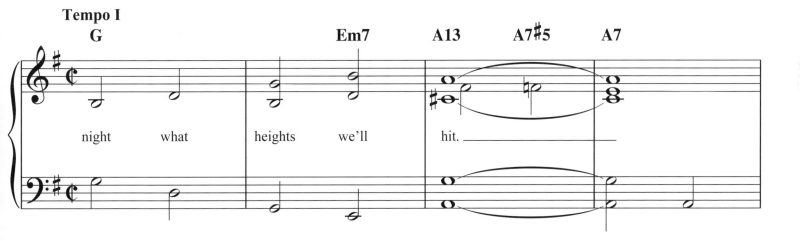

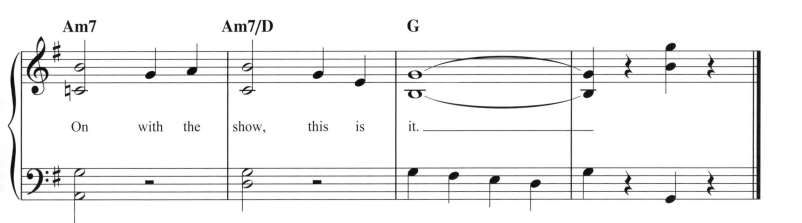

WALLACE AND GROMIT THEME

from WALLACE AND GROMIT

By JULIAN NOTT

March tempo

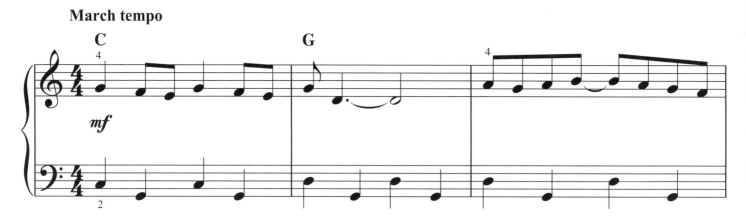

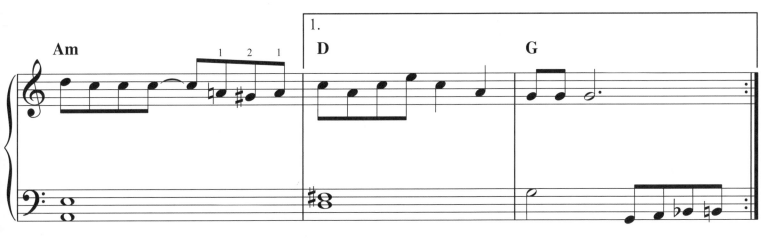

WOODY WOODPECKER
from the Cartoon Television Series

Words and Music by GEORGE TIBBLES
and RAMEY IDRISS

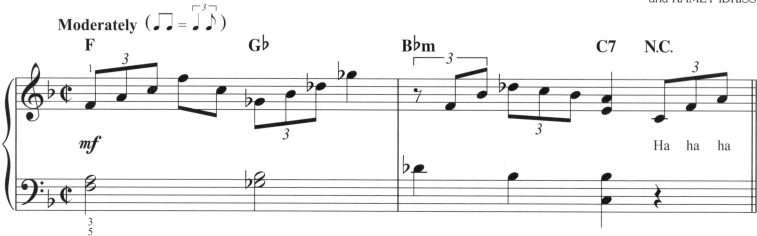

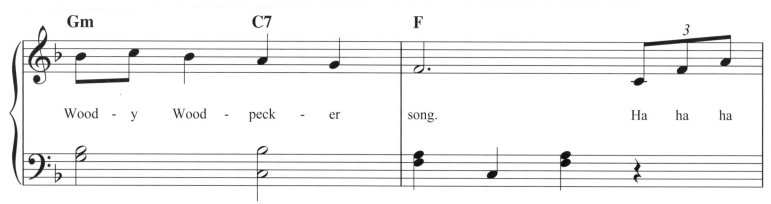

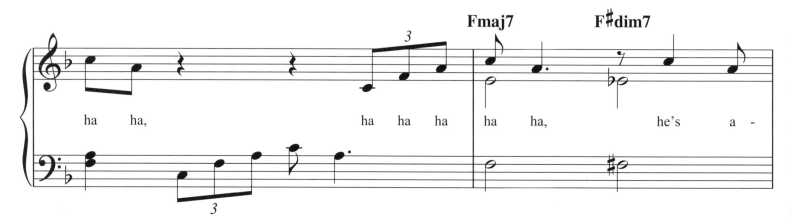

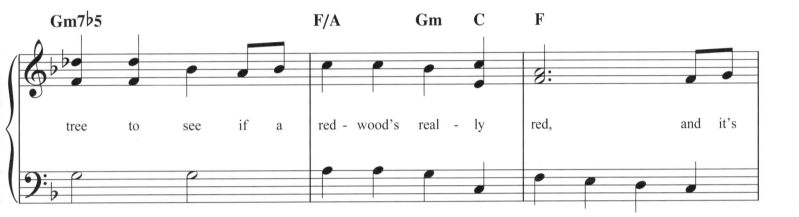

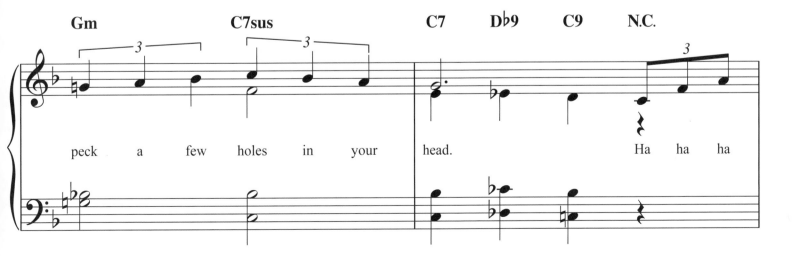

F   **Fmaj7**   **F#dim7**

ha   ha,   ha ha ha ha ha,   that's the

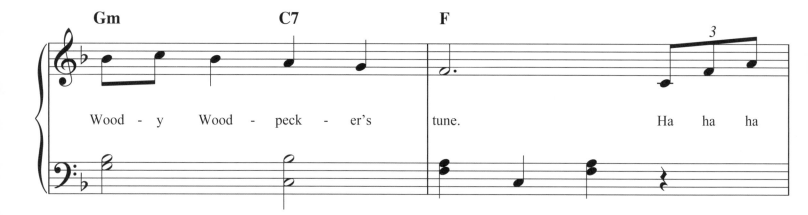

Gm   **C7**   **F**

Wood - y Wood - peck - er's   tune.   Ha ha ha

Fmaj7   **F#dim7**

ha   ha,   ha ha ha ha ha,   makes the

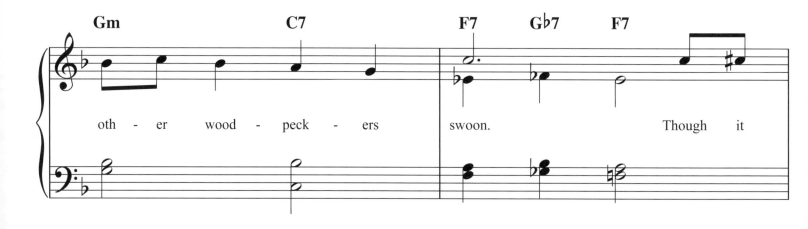

Gm   **C7**   **F7**   **G♭7**   **F7**

oth - er wood - peck - ers   swoon.   Though it

B♭ ... **Gm7♭5**

does-n't make sense to the dull and the dense, all the

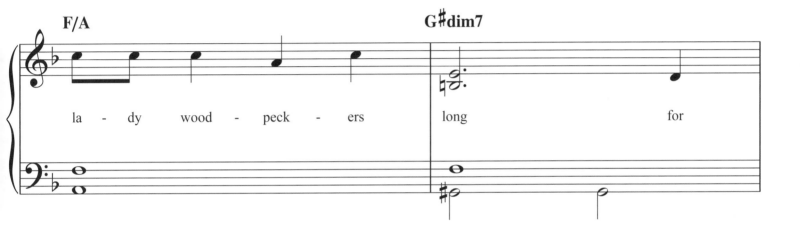

F/A ... **G♯dim7**

la — dy wood — peck — ers long for

F/A ... **D7**

ha ha ha ha ha, ha ha ha ha ha, that's the

G **C7** ‖1. **F** ‖2. **F**

Wood - y Wood - peck - er song. Ha ha ha song.

WINNIE THE POOH

from THE MANY ADVENTURES OF WINNIE THE POOH

Words and Music by RICHARD M. SHERMAN
and ROBERT B. SHERMAN

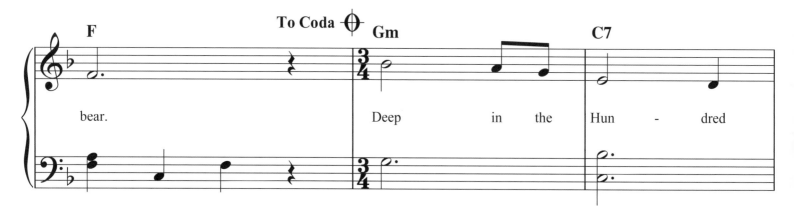

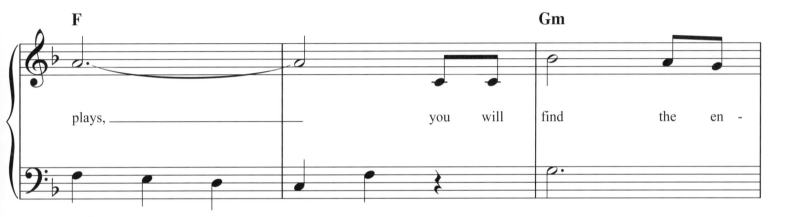

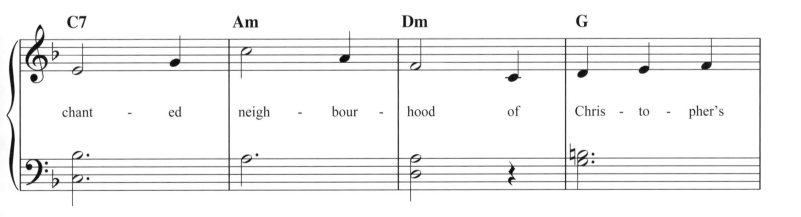

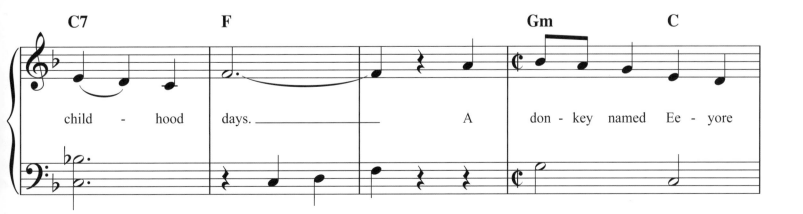

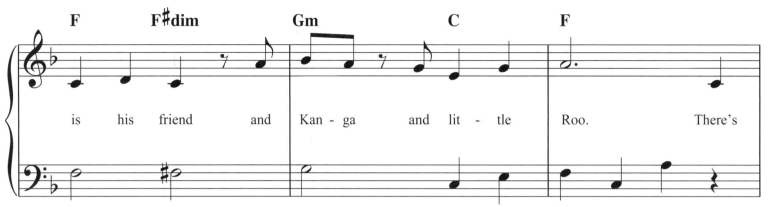

is his friend and Kan - ga and lit - tle Roo. There's

Rab - bit and Pig - let and there's Owl, but most of all, Win - nie the

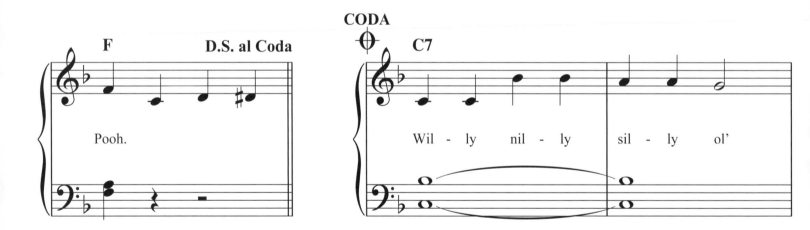

Pooh. Wil - ly nil - ly sil - ly ol'

bear.